Martin Luther King, Jr.

A Man to Remember

by Patricia McKissack

 CHILDRENS PRESS, CHICAGO

PICTURE ACKNOWLEDGMENTS

United Press International—2, 21, 40, 65, 66, 67, 68, 69, 70, 71, 80, 108, 116
Black Star—© Flip Schulke, 8, 59; © Charles Moorr, 64; © Bob Fitch, 101;
© Declan Haun, 103
© Karen Yops—20 (2 photos)
Historical Pictures Service, Chicago—47, 121

**Page 2—Reverend Martin Luther King with his two-year-old son, Martin
Luther King III, pulls up a four-foot cross that was burned on the
front lawn of his home on April 26, 1960.**

Page 8—Martin Luther King in his church in Atlanta.

Library of Congress Cataloging in Publication Data

McKissack, Pat, 1944-
  Martin Luther King, Jr., a man to remember.

  Bibliography: p.
  Includes index.
  Summary: A biography of the Baptist minister from
Georgia who led a non-violent crusade against racial
segregation which resulted in new awareness among
Americans of all colors of the principles on which their
nation was founded.
  1. King, Martin Luther—Juvenile literature.
2. Afro-Americans—Civil rights—Juvenile literature.
3. Afro-Americans—Biography—Juvenile literature.
4. Baptists—United States—Clergy—Biography—Juvenile
literature. [1. King, Martin Luther. 2. Civil rights workers.
3. Clergy. 4. Afro-Americans—Biography] I. Title.
E185.97.K5M36 1984   323.4'092'4 [B] [92] 83-23933
ISBN 0-516-03206-2

11 12 13 14 15 16 17 18 19 R 02 01 00 99 98 97 96 95

DEDICATION

To my many Mamas:
> Mama Frances
> Mama Sarah
> Mary Virginia
> Mom Bessye
> My Mother, Erma

Table of Contents

Introduction

THAT'S JUST THE WAY IT IS

*"For years the Negro had heard
the word 'Wait!' and 'Wait'
had nearly always meant 'Never!'"*

"Letter from a Birmingham Jail"
written by Martin Luther King, Jr.

Atlanta, Georgia, 1935—

The people who lived on Auburn Street were accustomed to hearing the squeals and shouts of two growing boys at play. One boy, a black child, was the son of a Baptist minister; the other, a white child, was the son of a grocery store owner.

The young boys had been playmates for as long as either of them could remember. They had spent hours playing the games that children play. Side by side they had fought fire-breathing dragons, escaped the attacks of sword-wielding pirates, and visited faraway places on a magical carpet.

Without anybody's really noticing, these boys had shared one of the most important periods of growing up. Then, on a September day in 1935, the friendship came to an abrupt end. Both boys had just started school—separate schools—and the parents of the white child figured it was time for the children to be separated in play as well.

No more playing together. . . ever!

"But, why?" asked the black child.

"Because we are white and you are colored," he was told. "Sorry, but that's just the way it is." And that was the way it was at that time in America's Southland.

The black child was too hurt to be angry, too confused to be bitter. He wanted an answer. He just couldn't understand how the color of his skin could be the cause of a wrecked friendship. He would soon learn the awful truth—that it was *just* the color of his skin that had made the difference.

While growing up, this child was called M.L. But, by age of thirty-five, he was internationally known as The Reverend Dr. Martin Luther King, Jr. As a child, M.L. had asked—Why couldn't white and black people work together, pray together, shop together, eat together, ride buses and trains together, play together, and live together in peace and brotherly love? As an adult Dr. King was still asking—Why?

Finally, Martin Luther King concluded that there was no real reason for segregation and race hatred in a country founded on the principles of justice and equality for all citizens. So, he began asking another question. It caused Americans of all colors to look inside their hearts to find the answer to the old problem of race discrimination.

When segregationists argued, "But that's just the way it is," Dr. King asked, "But is that the way it should be?"

Millions of Americans responded with an overwhelming "No!"

Chapter 1

REMEMBERING. . .

Once riding in Old Baltimore
Heart-filled, head-filled with glee,
I saw a Baltimorian
Keep looking straight at me.

Now I was eight and very small,
And he was no whit bigger,
And so I smiled, but he poked out
His tongue and called me, "Nigger!"

I saw the whole of Baltimore
From May until December;
Of all the things that happened there,
That's all that I remember.

"Incident" from *On These I Stand: An Anthology of the Best Poems of Countee Cullen.*

Martin Luther King, Jr. was born on a cold and cloudy Saturday, January 15, 1929. Daddy King wanted his first son to be named after him. Since everybody called the father Mike, the doctor assumed his name was Michael and wrote Michael King, Jr. on the baby's birth certificate. To offset the error, everybody called the baby M.L. It wasn't until M.L. joined church at the age of five that Daddy King officially corrected both their names to Martin Luther King, Sr. and Jr. It didn't change anything; everybody still called the father Mike and the son M.L.

Little M.L. grew up a happy child, bright-eyed, full of fun, and "smart as a whip," his grandmother always said. He loved the big rooms in the house on Auburn Street; they always smelled of good things to eat, and eating was what made M.L. the happiest. Sunday dinners were his favorite— fried chicken, candied sweet potatoes, black-eyed peas cooked with ham hocks, and peach cobbler. The food was always well prepared and perfectly seasoned. Southern blacks would have said that whenever M.L.'s mother cooked, she "put her foot in the pot."

M.L. always felt safe at 501 Auburn Street. The old Victorian house had belonged to his grandparents, the Williamses. His mother had grown up in it. When his parents married, they had come to live in the house. M.L. had been born in the Auburn Street house, as had his elder sister— Willie Christine—and his little brother—Alfred Daniel, known to all as A.D.. The Auburn Street house was big enough for three generations of the King and the Williams family to live, love, and learn in.

Three blocks away was M.L.'s second home, the Ebenezer Baptist Church, where Daddy King was the pastor. M.L. was young, but he knew that his family and Ebenezer Baptist Church shared one proud history.

M.L.'s mother, Alberta Williams King, was the daughter of Alfred Daniel Williams, who pastored Ebenezer Baptist from 1894 until his death in 1931. Like other ministers of his day, the Reverend Alfred Williams was a civic leader who used his position to speak out against the injustices of segregation and racism. Rev. Williams was one of the first members of the National Association for the Advancement of Colored People (NAACP) and helped to get Booker T. Washington High School built, the first black high school in Atlanta.

Alfred Williams was an educated man, but he enjoyed using the language of the common folk. Some of his church members didn't share their pastor's admiration for black language. A favorite family story tells about one of grandfather Williams's parishioners, who insisted upon correcting the minister's grammatical errors. One Sunday after the collection had been counted, Williams said to the worrisome member, "I done give a hundred dollars, but the gentleman who corrected me has given nothing." That was the end of that.

Grandfather Williams was a hardworking, self-made man, who was a loving and dedicated husband and father. He tried to protect his family from the cruelties he had experienced because of racism. Living in Atlanta helped to make this possible to some degree.

Nashville and Atlanta were considered the "best" of the southern cities; there blacks were not subjected to some of the harsher circumstances of segregation found in the rural South. These two cities were the southern black educational centers, and a small group of well-educated professionals lived there in relative comfort.

Rev. Alfred Williams took advantage of the educational opportunities available to black Atlantans and sent his daughter, Alberta, to the best schools. Alberta was a fine musician who taught school until she married, quite an accomplishment for a southern lady of color in the late 1920s.

Mother Dear (the name the King children called their mother) had come from a well-educated, respected family. But Daddy King (the name the King children called their father) had come from a poor, uneducated family. He had had to struggle to accomplish everything he did.

M.L. liked hearing his father tell stories about growing up in rural Georgia. Most of his young life, Daddy King had spent behind a plow mule. "I may have smelled like a mule," Daddy King would shout, "but I didn't think like a mule."

M.L. also loved to hear his father talk about his parents.

"My mother," Daddy King would begin, "wanted to name me Michael after the archangel, and my father wanted to name me Martin Luther after his two brothers. They couldn't decide, so they compromised and called me Mike."

Mike King's father drank; his mother worked long, hard hours cooking and cleaning for the local banker. Young Mike took all he could of sharecropping and at age fifteen, he decided to leave home.

Shaking the dust of that town off his feet, he headed for Atlanta. But, before he left town, Mike stood in the shadow of the banker's house and promised himself that one day he would own a two-story brick home and a bank too! If anybody had overheard this poor, raggedy black child making such a wild promise, they would have thought him either silly or sick. But they didn't know Mike King.

Once he reached Atlanta, Mike started working to make his dreams a reality. During the day he worked at odd jobs, and at night he attended school. He believed education was the key to a better life. It took Daddy King eleven years to earn his high school diploma, but he did it! That meant something to him. He didn't have to "take low" for any man.

It was during this time that Mike met his future father-in-law, Rev. Alfred Williams. The elderly pastor of Ebenezer greatly influenced his young friend's decision to preach. He encouraged this industrious young man to further his education in the ministry.

M.L. loved to hear his father tell how he and Mother Dear met and married. While visiting Rev. Williams, Mike met Alberta. He immediately told some of his friends that he was going to marry her. Soon it was clear who Mike King was coming to visit on Auburn Street. After a "proper" courtship, Alberta and Mike were married on Thanksgiving Day, 1926. Mike became the assistant pastor of Ebenezer and continued to work on his degree in divinity from Morehouse College, which Grandfather Williams had attended.

Daddy King demanded respect, and everybody knew it. M.L. never saw his father shuffle his feet in front of white folk, and it made a difference in how he saw himself. M.L. began to believe as his father. . . "I am somebody."

After Rev. Alfred D. Williams died, Mike became pastor of Ebenezer. Because of his outspoken nature, he became a community leader and a spokesman for the black cause as well. Black pride was practically unheard of at this time, and any black who stood up for his rights was accused of being "uppity." In Atlanta, as in other parts of the South, a black man who dared to stand up to a white was called a "crazy nigger" and was brutally beaten or sometimes murdered by a lynch mob. Being "uppity" in the South could get you killed.

Mother Dear feared for her husband, but he always told her, "You can't be afraid of doing what's right."

M.L. remembered that his father did try to right the

wrongs he saw. If he took the family downtown, he never went to the back of the store to shop. He never went to the back of the line if there were white customers waiting behind him. He looked white men in the eye and passed Georgia's very difficult and unfair literacy test to earn the right to vote in national elections. In 1936 he led a voting rights march to the doors of Atlanta's City Hall.

M.L. had quite a father!

M.L. had quite a family!

Grandfather Williams and Daddy King were proud, positive-thinking black men. Mother Dear was a refined woman with character. She and Daddy King taught their children the importance of self-pride. "You are as good as any man," they said.

Being Mike King's son had its advantages. Daddy King loved his children; they had everything they needed and a lot of things they wanted. Many people accused him of loving his children too much. Mike King took pride in having overcome poverty and enjoyed giving his family many of the material things he didn't have as a child. But, there was a limit to his indulgence. Daddy King was a taskmaster. He was head of the King household, and he would not tolerate the slightest disrespect. Misconduct was quickly punished with a good spanking. . . "One you won't forget."

The children knew the consequences of making their father angry. Christine rarely got spankings, but A.D.

stayed in trouble all the time. M.L. tried to stay out of trouble. It broke his heart whenever Daddy King had to spank him, but he stubbornly refused to cry.

Whenever M.L. got one of those Daddy King "you-won't-forget spankings," he ran to his grandmother, Mama Williams. (She was the one who cried when M.L. got a spanking.) Mama was M.L.'s favorite family member; he loved her dearly. She loved him too.

Everybody knew that M.L. was very close to his grandmother. But nobody realized how close until an incident that took place when M.L. was about seven or eight years old.

A.D. and M.L. liked to slide down the highly polished banister in the front hallway. They had been warned not to slide on it, since M.L. had taken a nasty fall when he was younger. Still the boys slid down the bannister whenever they thought no one was looking.

On one particular day, A.D. slid down and crashed into Mama who happened to be passing by. She was knocked out by the blow. M.L. saw his grandmother lying there on the floor. She was so still and quiet. Certain that she had been killed, he ran to his room and jumped out the window. M.L. survived the jump; Grandmother survived the bump. From that day, nothing was said about the incident, but everybody knew that M.L. was very, very attached to his grandmother.

The closeness with his grandmother grew because M.L. could share ideas with her that he wouldn't discuss with

Ebenezer Baptist Church   Birthplace of Martin Luther King

anyone else. He questioned things about church, but he didn't feel comfortable discussing them with Daddy King. He had heard his father preach many times about "loving your enemies." M.L., at that age, believed white people were enemies. He couldn't understand how he was expected to love a group of people who had shown how much they hated him. The whole idea worried him. He didn't like hating, but he didn't understand how he was to love either. Could he be a Christian feeling this way? Could he be a preacher feeling this way? Did he even *want* to be a preacher?

Sometimes those inner conflicts felt as though they were tearing him apart. That's when M.L. went to his Grandmother Williams. He sought her out because she was comforting and reassuring in her love. Mama never hated anybody; she was too full of kindness.

The family of Martin Luther King, Jr. From left, his mother, Mrs. Alberta Williams King; his father, Martin Luther King, Sr.; and his grandmother, Jennie Williams. In front are his younger brother, Alfred Daniel; his sister, Christine; and young Martin.

As long as M.L. lived on Auburn Street with Daddy King, Mother Dear, Christine, A.D., and Mama, his world was secure and comfortable. He was able to cope. Then things changed. It began when he was twelve. Mama died.

One day M.L. turned the corner of Auburn Street to find that a crowd had gathered outside his house. He was sure something bad had happened because he had sneaked away to see a parade on Sunday. God was punishing him, he thought. When he reached the porch, he was told his grandmother had died of a heart attack. Mama was dead! M.L. felt responsible; he wanted to die too.

He cried for days and hardly slept or ate. Nothing could take away the hurt he felt inside. Then, in time, his parents helped him accept the fact that Mama was gone. They made him understand that God didn't punish little boys but loved them. Still, he wasn't so sure about death. There were so many questions.

His parents realized that M.L. would have to work these questions out for himself. Daddy King and Mother Dear helped by telling the boy about God's plan for salvation, which all Christians are taught to believe. It helped M.L. to hear that Mama was in Heaven and that one day he would see her again. Holding on to this belief finally led him to accept his grandmother's death, but all his life he would feel the tremendous loss.

Shortly after Mama Williams died, Daddy King sold the family home. He bought a two-story brick house just like the one he had promised he would own one day. He was also, at that time, the director of a black-owned bank. Daddy King had fulfilled his dream.

When M.L. entered his teen years he had a strong legacy: a grandfather who had been a proud and dignified spokesman for the poor and oppressed; a warm, understanding grandmother; a well-educated mother; and a prosperous father, who was also an outspoken leader in the community. M.L. lived in a grand house, and his future was bright.

In the years to come, Martin Luther King, Jr. would often recall his earliest years and the happy memories of the old house on Auburn Street. It was in this house that the foundations for his life's work were laid.

Chapter 2

HATE THE SIN NOT THE SINNER

*"We must meet the forces of hate with
the power of love; we must meet physical
force with soul force."*

Quote from a speech given by Martin Luther King, Jr.

One of the best features of the new house on Boulevard Street was Daddy King's library. Mother Dear had taught all her children to read at an early age, but it was M.L. who enjoyed books the most. "Even before he could read, he kept books around him," remembered Daddy King. "He just liked the idea of having them."

M.L. was so bright that his parents had slipped him into school a year early. Within a week, however, M.L. had told the teacher his real age, so he was sent home to wait until the following year, when he could legitimately enroll in Yonge Street Elementary School.

The boy had sailed through school, skipping several grades as he progressed. He entered Booker T. Washington High School at the age of thirteen. It was 1942, the same year the Kings moved to the house on Boulevard Street.

In the fall of 1942 World War II was on everybody's mind. Black men were going off to war in segregated units, yet fighting for *freedom*. A. Philip Randolph, a black labor leader, threatened to lead a massive march to Washington if blacks weren't given jobs in the defense industry. Franklin D. Roosevelt responded by issuing a presidential order prohibiting racial discrimination in government defense plants. A new organization called the Congress of Racial Equality (CORE) led successful sit-ins in Chicago, New York, and other northern cities. But in the South, blacks were still living in a rigidly segregated society.

At age fourteen Martin stood 5 feet 7 inches, his adult height. He had a dark brown complexion, bright almond shaped eyes, and a baritone voice that seemed to add inches to his height. M.L. learned early in life that his voice was an asset. He learned to use it to impress his teachers and charm the girls.

During high school M.L. had many friends. He was an active swimmer and tennis player and belonged to the neighborhood baseball and football teams. A.D. was better at sports, but Martin was much more aggressive. His friends, who were nicknamed "Rooster," "Sack," and "Mole," were his "main buddies." One of M.L.'s nicknames was "Tweed" because he wore tweed suits. M.L. also had a street name, "Will Shoot," earned because he never failed to shoot the basketball *every time* it was passed to him.

Along with his sports trophies, M.L. acquired a good vocabulary. He loved words and enjoyed writing, even though he didn't spell well. M.L. managed to be "one of the guys," even though he was smart and used big words. His buddies didn't seem to mind. It was understood that preachers always used big words, and that's what everyone said M.L. was going to be. But Martin wasn't so sure about that!

Martin enjoyed debating and speaking before an audience. In the eleventh grade, he entered an oratorical contest sponsored by the Negro Elks. He and his teacher went to the contest, which was held in a town just outside Atlanta.

M.L.'s topic was "The Negro and the Constitution," and his presentation won him a prize. He had such a good feeling! That night, when he and his teacher started for home on a bus, they were so busy enjoying the excitement of the victory that they didn't notice the bus was filling up. Suddenly the driver stopped the bus and walked to the back. He told Martin and his teacher they had to give up their seats to white passengers. Martin refused to obey the bus driver or his teacher. Anger had filled him with defiance. Then the bus driver swore at M.L. and threatened him. M.L. wasn't frightened of the bus driver, but when he saw that his teacher was near tears, he gave up his seat for her sake. Martin rode the rest of the way home in silence.

In the spring of 1944, M.L. took and passed the college entrance examination. He graduated from Washington High after the eleventh grade and enrolled in Morehouse College in Atlanta. M.L. was fifteen years old.

That summer, before entering Morehouse, Martin was sent to work on a tobacco farm in Connecticut. It was his first time away from the South and he loved the freedom— freedom from the restraints of segregation. In Hartford he could enter a movie through the front door and sit *anywhere* he wanted, even in a front row seat. It was nice not having to worry about being in his "proper place." Although the work was hard, M.L. hated to see summer end. It was difficult returning to the segregated South.

Coming home on the train, M.L. went to the dining car, where he was seated and served like everybody else. Later on he went back to the diner, but this time the waiter escorted him to a back seat. A curtain was drawn around him so he could not be seen. That was his harsh reminder that the train had crossed the Virginia border. Segregation laws were in practice again. Many years later, Martin Luther King wrote that the curtain was like a wall being pulled down on his "personhood." He decided that whatever he did in life, it had to help change segregation. He felt no person should have to feel such humiliation.

The Morehouse years were good ones for Martin. Daddy King was still pushing him to be a minister, but being a lawyer sounded much more appealing. He selected sociology as his major and English as his minor. Morehouse had some of the most outstanding educators and scholars of that day and they helped to influence young Martin's life. Professors like Dr. Walter Chivers, Dr. Gladstone Lewis Chandler, and Dr. George D. Kelsey helped to guide his academic career.

Dr. Kelsey helped Martin sort out many doubts he had about religion. Martin was amazed to find that he was encouraged—almost expected—to challenge ideas, read differing opinions, and compare the writings of many writers. He learned that questioning did not show a lack of faith. Questioning helped him to seek, and it was through the search that he would learn to express, with confidence, what he did believe. With his thoughts out in the open, Martin realized that his faith was a very important part of his life.

Dr. Benjamin Mays, president of Morehouse College, was a family friend who was also a progressive minister. He helped Martin see the role of a minister differently. Dr. Mays was proud of the Morehouse tradition. "Do whatever you do so well," Mays told his student body, "that no man living and no man yet unborn can do it better." Mays proudly proclaimed that the Morehouse tradition was not to turn out mere scholars, but men.

Martin was very impressed with the Morehouse faculty— especially Dr. Mays. The Morehouse philosophy of excellence and the Morehouse history of service to the community changed his whole concept of the ministry, and by age seventeen Martin felt "called" to be a minister.

When M.L. told Daddy King his decision, his father gave him his first assignment. He was to preach his first sermon at Ebenezer. M.L. agreed, and his first sermon was a tremendous success. Daddy King was proud!

Between preparing for Sunday services and dating as many girls as was "acceptable," Martin worked as a laborer during the summers. When the foreman insisted upon calling M.L. a nigger every time he did something wrong, he quit. It was later on that he realized that he had been able to quit the job, but what about those men who couldn't? It must be awful having to work under those conditions, he thought.

Back at Morehouse, Martin discussed his work experiences with his professors. He began to realize how privileged he was to get an education. But with that privilege came a responsibility to those who weren't getting the same opportunity. As an educated black man, Martin felt he should use his education to help less fortunate blacks.

But how? At the time the idea of social ministry was not a new idea, but it certainly was not widely accepted. Martin did not want to be a minister who talked only about Heaven and didn't apply the message of the Gospels to daily life and problem solving. Martin believed that the Gospels, put into practice, helped people live a better life here on earth.

While in school, Martin studied the writings of many scholars and philosophers. He was especially interested in American black leaders. He read about Nat Turner, who led a slave uprising in the early 1800s. He read the writings of Frederick Douglass, the former slave who spoke eloquently for the cause of freed slaves. There was Booker T. Washington, who advocated accepting segregation and working hard to better oneself through education. Then there was W.E.B. Du Bois, who disagreed with Washington. *What good did it do*, asked Du Bois, *to learn a skill and then be denied the right to practice it?* Du Bois advocated fighting for freedom in the courts and was the cofounder of the NAACP in 1909. (The NAACP won its first court battle in 1918, the same year the modern Ku Klux Klan was formed on Stone Mountain in Georgia.) Finally, there was Marcus Garvey, who had formed a "Back to Africa" movement that had not succeeded.

Martin was still looking for answers when he graduated from Morehouse in the spring of 1948. That same year his sister, Christine, graduated from Spelman, a school for black women in Atlanta. After Morehouse, Martin decided to study for a degree in divinity at Crozer Seminary in Chester, Pennsylvania.

Crozer was located on the banks of the Delaware River, just outside Philadelphia. It was an ideal place to study and learn. Only one hundred students were in his class, among them twelve women and six blacks.

At first Martin was tense. Living around whites for the first time made him uncomfortable. All his life he'd heard the stereotypes: blacks were supposed to laugh at anything; they never washed; they were always late; and they were always loud and wrong. Martin went to the opposite extreme, putting unreasonable restrictions on himself. He rarely laughed; he kept his room spotless, his clothing perfect, his shoes highly polished, and his body immaculately clean; and he was always early for appointments and class. In addition he studied hard and earned straight A's. During that first semester at Crozer, Martin was at the top of his class, but he was remembered as being very "tight."

Actually, Martin wasn't the stuffed shirt everybody

thought he was. He had an outlet. Whenever he could, he enjoyed himself dating, dancing, and dazzling eligible young ladies with his impressive vocabulary.

After he had been at Crozer for a while, he began to feel a little more relaxed. He made friends more easily and enjoyed socializing with the other students. But again, he was to be reminded that racism was everywhere.

Martin was in his dormitory room studying one evening when someone knocked. He answered. There stood a student from North Carolina, who had made his dislike for "Nigras" known. The student accused Martin of messing up his room. He cursed Martin, then threatened him with a gun. Martin showed no fear. He calmly explained to his accuser that he knew nothing about the room raid. By that time, students had begun gathering outside in the hallway. When they saw the North Carolina student with a gun, they forced him to put it away and leave. The incident was reported immediately, but Martin refused to press charges and asked that the incident be forgotten. Crozer faculty and students forced the North Carolinian to apologize to Martin publicly. Martin became well liked and respected by both faculty and students for the way in which he had handled himself. It took courage to do what he had done. In the end even the North Carolinian became a friend.

During his Crozer years, Martin continued to study the world philosophers. Then, quite by accident, he stumbled onto the one philosophy that would help him identify his life's work.

Dr. Mordecai Johnson, president of Howard University, a university for blacks in Washington, D.C., came to Crozer to speak about his recent trip to India. Martin had nothing else to do; it was free; so he decided to attend Dr. Johnson's lecture.

The subject was Mohandas Gandhi. Martin sat on the edge of his chair listening to the life and teachings of Gandhi, the Indian leader who had *nonviolently* helped to free India from British colonialism. Gandhi had also attacked India's caste system, which restricted Untouchables (those at the bottom of the caste system) from government or social participation. While upper-class Indians lived in splendor, millions of Untouchables and other lower-class Indians were starving. Gandhi called the system unjust and protested these injustices by ridding himself of all his personal wealth. He fasted; he prayed; he demonstrated.

Gandhi's "Soul Force," the power of love, had given Martin the basis for positive change. He was too excited to talk; he wanted to read. All along, Christianity had taught him "Love your enemy." But Martin had had problems with understanding how to love a person who hated him. He wanted to know more about Gandhi; he was led to Thoreau. The more he read, the more excited he became.

In Henry David Thoreau's essay "Civil Disobedience," he

was introduced to the vehicle through which he could display his dissatisfaction with a system and *still* remain true to his Christian beliefs. Thoreau believed man should not obey laws and customs that were not just, laws and customs that harmed a man's spirit or his body. So did Gandhi. So did Christ.

Martin had his answer. Hate the sin, not the sinner. Attack the wrong, not the person doing the wrong. Martin was overjoyed. He had found the weapon that could bring about positive changes. It wasn't anything new or original. Love was the answer; nonviolent protest was the vehicle.

Chapter 3

DIXIE-BOUND

The glory of the day was in her face,
The beauty of the night was in her eyes.
And over all her loveliness, the grace
of Morning blushing in the early skies.

And in her voice, the calling of the dove;
like music of a sweet, melodious part.
And in her smile, the breaking light of love;
And all the gentle virtues in her heart.

From "St. Peter Relates an Incident"
by James Weldon Johnson.

Martin Luther King, Jr. graduated from Crozer Seminary in June 1951, with a B.A. degree in divinity. Seeing Martin finish at the top of his class and receive a $1,300 scholarship to further his studies made Daddy King and Mother Dear the "proudest parents in the world." Now Martin was expected to return to Atlanta, settle down, marry a well-respected girl, and take over the assistant pastorship of Ebenezer Baptist Church.

But, Martin wasn't ready for that yet. He agreed to spend his vacation in Atlanta and deliver most of the summer sermons at Ebenezer. He made it clear that in the fall he was going to Boston University to study for a Ph.D. In mid-September 1951, Martin left for Boston in his graduation gift—a shiny new green Chevrolet. It was Daddy King's way of saying, "I approve—go with my love and blessings."

Martin quickly adjusted to Boston University's rigorous academic requirements. He even took courses simultaneously at Harvard. Martin felt privileged to study under such progressive theologians as Dr. Edgar Sheffield Brightman and Dr. L. Harold DeWolf, who was his adviser. DeWolf respected King's scholarship and remembered him as being a serious minded, well-prepared young man.

Martin didn't spend *all* his time studying. He was disciplined enough to be able to have a good time and still maintain a well-deserved "A" average. He enjoyed balancing the best of both worlds. After delivering a brilliant paper in class, for example, he would go to the local soul food restaurant and enjoy a plate of chitlins and corn bread. He could debate a difficult philosophical subject and then go to a club and dance until the band went home.

Philip Lenud, a fellow Morehouse graduate who was a divinity student at Tufts University, became Martin's best friend. Philip shared his friend's love of soul food, dancing, and pretty girls. He and Martin enjoyed ranking girls according to their physical beauty, from "heavy" to "light," a heavy being a real beauty, a light being only so-so. Philip and Martin got along so well that they decided to share a four-room bachelor apartment.

By his second semester at Boston, Martin was beginning to tire of the playboy life. He asked a friend, "Do you know a nice girl from down home?"

Martin's friend gave him the number of an Alabama girl, Coretta Scott, who was a student at the New England Conservatory of Music in Boston. He listened with interest as she was described as "really smart and very pretty," a real *heavy*. Martin felt sure that this was a young woman he wanted to meet. "She doesn't like preachers," warned his friend. "She thinks they're all stuck up and full of a lot of hot air."

That didn't discourage Martin. On a cold February evening, he took a chance and called Miss Scott. After introducing himself as Martin King, he confidently asked her for a date. Then he added his usual line of flattery, "Your beauty is my Napoleon; I am your Waterloo."

"What?" said Coretta. "Don't be silly. You haven't met me yet." Flattery had always worked for him, but not with Coretta. Martin couldn't wait to meet her.

From the first, Martin knew Coretta Scott was not a girl he would date and forget. Coretta's first impression of Martin King was not so favorable. "After a while he became interesting," she told a writer years later, "especially when he stopped all that jive talk."

Before their first date was over, Martin had proposed. "You have all the qualities I want in a wife," he said. Coretta wasn't sure he was serious and if he was, she was doubly unsure about becoming a preacher's wife. There were too many dos and don'ts attached to the position. Also, she had worked too hard to become a concert singer to give it all up to be an acceptable preacher's wife. . .and a southern preacher's wife at that.

Coretta had some unpleasant memories of Alabama, where she had been born and raised. Her father's business and home had been burned because he refused to sell his thriving lumber company to a white man. She knew how hard it was to be a parent in the segregated South. Her own parents had tried to give her self-respect and dignity, only to see discrimination erode their efforts. She knew in her own life how hard it was to keep a positive self-image in a segregated society. She wasn't so sure she wanted to go "back down there" to live.

As much as she argued with herself, in the end her heart won; she agreed to become Mrs. Coretta Scott King. Daddy King married them on the lawn of Coretta's home in Marion, Alabama, on June 18, 1953. Martin's brother, A.D., was the best man.

The newlyweds returned to Boston and set up housekeeping in a four-room apartment. Coretta finished her studies at the conservatory and Martin finished his Ph.D. course work. Since he could write his thesis anywhere, he decided to take a job.

Everybody had an opinion about the job he should take. DeWolf was in favor of Martin's accepting one of the teaching offers he had received. A clear advantage of teaching was the opportunity to do more research and study. But after talking it over with Coretta, Martin decided to look for a pastorship of a church. (He felt he had been "called" to be a preacher and now that call had to be fulfilled.)

Coretta agreed with his decision, but encouraged him to look for a pastorship of a northern church, where she might be able to perform on the stage and not be condemned by his church members. But the firmest offer came from the membership of Dexter Avenue Baptist Church in Montgomery, Alabama. Coretta was not the least bit excited, but she tried not to be discouraging.

In January 1954 Martin went to the capital of Alabama, where he delivered such an inspiring sermon that he convinced the Dexter congregation he was the pastor they wanted and needed. By March, the congregation had made him a firm offer. As was their practice, Martin and Coretta discussed it before any decision was made. He knew her feelings about returning to the South; but he also knew how much she loved him. She would go if he insisted, but was it fair to ask her?

Coretta listened to her husband talk about the Dexter Avenue Baptist Church. His eyes sparkled when he talked about the small brick church with white doors and a steeple. Yes, if she insisted, he wouldn't take the pastorship; but she knew how important it was to him.

After talking about the pros and cons, they decided to go. "Oh, it'll just be for two, maybe three years," he said. "Then I'll take a job in the North."

That was a comfortable conclusion for both of them at the time. But, somehow they knew they were going *home* and wouldn't be coming back. Both of them felt an indefinable commitment to the South. They wanted to return and somehow better the conditions under which blacks lived. Neither one of them knew just how they were going to do it.

When Daddy King heard about the commitment, he was not impressed. "Montgomery!" he shouted. "Why in the world would you—or anybody for that matter—want to go

Martin Luther King, Sr. was pastor of the Ebenezer Baptist Church for forty-four years.

there to live?" (In the mid-1950s blacks were leaving Alabama and Mississippi as fast as they could to get away from the extreme and intolerable racism.) No matter how much Daddy King fumed and fussed, the younger Kings were Dixie-bound. They were on their way to Montgomery, Alabama, the capital of the Confederacy, "The Heart of Dixie."

As it happened, Martin and Coretta were returning to the

South with something to be optimistic about. In May 1954, the United States Supreme Court ruled segregated schools unconstitutional and ordered all public schools integrated. In one blow the Supreme Court had smashed the "separate but equal" doctrine and the legal system that protected it.

Blacks all over the South rejoiced. Some states grudgingly accepted the ruling and integrated the school systems. But, the Dixie states found a loophole. No time frame had been given. The Supreme Court then ordered that schools be desegregated "with all deliberate speed." Southern states interpreted that to mean as fast as they felt like going. "These things take time," said one southern school official. "We're working on it. . . it'll get done. . . one of these days." There were only scattered cases of a southern judge's ordering a school to integrate. In spite of the ruling, most southern schools stayed segregated.

Segregationists responded angrily to any civil rights legislation. "There'll never be any integration in the South— ever!" they shouted. White Citizens Councils began forming; Ku Klux Klan membership increased.

Still, Martin and Coretta were hopeful. In May 1954 Rev. Martin Luther King, Jr. preached his first sermon as the pastor of Dexter Avenue Baptist Church. By September the Kings had settled down in a seven-room frame house. Coretta began making it a home. Martin began pastoring his church. Martin and Coretta had come home.

Chapter 4

BUSES, BOMBS, AND BOYCOTTS

She even thinks that up in heaven,
Her class lies late and snores
While poor black cherubs rise at seven
To do celestial chores.

"For a Lady I Know" from *On These I Stand:*
An Anthology of the Best Poems of Countee Cullen.
Copyright 1925 by Harper & Row, Publishers, Inc.; renewed 1953 by
Ida M. Cullen. Reprinted by permission of the publisher.

The friendship between the Reverend Ralph Abernathy and the Reverend Martin Luther King, Jr. began almost immediately after the Kings moved to Montgomery. Since Abernathy had grown up in Montgomery, he was able to help King adjust to his new home.

On more than one occasion, King and Abernathy discussed the Supreme Court's school desegregation order and what the ruling meant to southern blacks. Were changes about to take place? Neither of them believed that any social changes would come to the South very soon. "Alabama will be the last state in the Union to accept desegregation," said Abernathy, who understood how viciously the segregationists in Alabama had fought to protect the "southern way of life."

King believed that change would come hard, too. He decided that the best way he could help was to make his church members more aware of the things they could do to help themselves. Beyond that, he really had no plans to become a leader of any movement.

Then on December 1, 1955, Mrs. Rosa Parks, a seamstress who worked in a downtown department store, boarded a bus. Forever after, the lives of millions would be altered, including those of Rev. Ralph Abernathy and Rev. and Mrs. Martin Luther King, Jr.

Mrs. Parks had worked hard; she was tired. After paying her money to board the bus, she found a seat in the back section. As she rode along, she didn't notice that the bus was filling up or that a few white passengers were standing. The driver noticed, however, and stopped the bus. He ordered Mrs. Parks to give her seat to a white man who was standing. "No," said Mrs. Parks. She refused to move and calmly explained that she had paid her money the same as the other bus passengers. That gave her the *right* to be seated. But that's not the way it was in Montgomery, the bus driver informed Mrs. Parks. She had no such rights; she was breaking the law.

Rosa Parks was a small, neatly dressed woman whose poise and quiet manner caught the bus driver off guard. He decided to let the police handle her. Mrs. Parks was arrested, taken to jail, and booked for violating a Montgomery city ordinance.

Pullman porter E.D. Nixon, a black labor leader and social activist, and Mrs. Jo Ann Robinson of the Women's Political Council, along with local leaders of the NAACP, rallied behind Mrs. Parks. They quickly planned a one-day bus boycott to protest her arrest.

The Montgomery bus drivers had a reputation for being merciless in their treatment of black passengers, and the various black leaders had been looking for a good solid reason to boycott. Mrs. Parks was not the first person to be arrested, but she was the first person who had an impeccable record and a flawless character. She had no prior arrests and was a hardworking woman, a pillar of the black community. The NAACP thought hers was a case they could take all the way to the Supreme Court to test the legality of segregation laws on public facilities.

While the city's black activists worked to plan a one-day boycott, black ministers were contacted all over Montgomery to help support it. When Rev. Dr. Martin Luther King was called, he was a bit apprehensive. His and Coretta's first child, Yolanda, had just been born on October 15, 1955. As a new father and a new pastor, he felt his first responsibilities were to his family and congregation. He also wondered if a boycott was morally right. Then he remembered a phrase from Henry David Thoreau's essay, "Civil Disobedience": "We can no longer lend our cooperation to an evil system." Not only was the bus boycott morally right, King felt obligated to be a part of it. He readily gave his support.

Leaflets had been passed out scheduling the boycott for Monday, December 5, 1955. That Sunday every black pastor in Montgomery encouraged his congregation not to ride the buses the next day. Instead they were to walk or ride in black-owned cabs, whose drivers had agreed to charge ten cents, the same as bus fare. Those blacks who owned cars were asked to form car pools.

In 1955 there were 48,000 blacks living in Montgomery; 75 percent of them rode the bus regularly. But, on the morning of December 5, only eight were seen riding a city bus. The organizers were delighted.

That afternoon Mrs. Rosa Parks appeared for a brief trial. She was, of course, found guilty and was fined ten dollars and four dollars court costs. Fred D. Gray, the NAACP lawyer, immediately informed the judge that the decision would be appealed. By fining Mrs. Parks, the judge had made it possible to appeal all the way to the Supreme Court, which is what the NAACP wanted to do. Victory No. 2.

Late that Monday evening, the boycott organizers voted to continue the bus strike. Victory No. 3. The successful one-day boycott had set a model. Spirits were high. The Montgomery Improvement Association (MIA) was formed to be the permanent committee that would carry out the planning and organization of the longer strike. Much to his surprise, Dr. King was nominated and unanimously elected president of the organization. He accepted the position graciously. Little did he know, at that time, in what a dangerous position he had placed himself and his family.

For the moment, Dr. King felt charged with enthusiasm. As the first president of the newly formed organization, he was expected to speak to the black population who had gathered at the Holt Street Church to hear what was going on. Already the people were asking, "What do we do now?" The success of the one-day strike had given them courage, hope to go on. There had been no time to prepare a speech, so, at the young age of twenty-six, Rev. Dr. Martin Luther King, Jr. stood before a packed house and spoke from his

Rosa Parks with Martin Luther King in the background

heart. What he said reflected his nonviolent beliefs and Christian heritage.

"In our protest," he began, "there will be no cross burnings. No white person will be taken from his home by a hooded Negro mob and brutally murdered," chanted King.

"Amen," responded the audience.

"There will be no threats and intimidation.... Our actions must be guided by the deepest principles of our Christian faith. Love must be our regulating ideal."

"Yes, Lord," the people shouted. "Praise the Lord."

King's voice flowed in the rhythmic style that was to become uniquely his own. "We must hear the words of Jesus echoing across the centuries: '*Love* your enemies, *bless* them that curse you, and *pray* for them that despitefully use you.'"

By the time King had finished, the shouts of praise had risen to a deafening pitch, accompanied with the traditional

"Amen, Amen." There was no doubt that the people of Montgomery had accepted Rev. Martin Luther King's leadership. They were ready to follow wherever he led them.

Amid the notes of an inspiring spiritual, Ralph Abernathy stepped to the platform. From the beginning, there was always a striking contrast between the two men. King was polished in his delivery, selecting each word for its importance and impact upon his listeners. Abernathy was earthy. He liked homespun phrases such as, "We won't give up the fight until we are as free to walk the streets of Montgomery as a jaybird is in whistling time." It was an effective contrast that formed a strong working relationship and a binding friendship between King and Abernathy.

That night at Holt Street Church, Ralph Abernathy stepped to the pulpit and presented the conditions of the boycott. There were three demands: (1) courteous treatment, (2) seating on a first-come, first-served basis, and (3) black bus drivers in predominantly black routes. "We will not stop until we have been given these basic rights," Abernathy called out. Everyone agreed. "Amen!"

The bus strike continued. At first Montgomery officials called the demands outrageous and a Communist plot to overthrow the country. "Every time a black man gets an idea to fight for his rights," one black boycotter said, "the white people claim it is a Communist plot. Communists are white; why should we expect better treatment from them?"

The mayor of Montgomery ignored the boycott, but the downtown merchants couldn't ignore their losses. Since the boycott was definitely having an impact on downtown trade, business owners took matters into their own hands. They began telling their black employees that if they participated in the bus strike, they would be fired. In response, many black workers quit their jobs rather than quit the boycott.

By the end of the first month, city officials showed a willingness to talk, but the meeting ended when neither side felt the other was listening. When negotiations failed, the city tried harrassment. The black cab companies were threatened with loss of their licenses because their permits contained a minimum fee charge of sixty cents. To protect themselves, the cab companies had to withdraw their services.

When news of the harrassment spread, the boycotters got stronger. They vowed not to ride the buses again until their demands were met. The MIA doubled its efforts to organize car pools. Undertakers volunteered funeral cars to transport people to and from work. Doctors, lawyers—anybody with a car and flexible working hours—joined the car pools, providing people with rides to and from work.

Then there were those who chose to walk. An elderly lady was offered a ride, but she refused, saying, "I'm not walking for myself. I'm walking for my children and grandchildren." That grandmother reflected the spirit of the boycott.

The longer the strike lasted, the more pressure was placed

on the organizers and leaders. Police harrassment continued. Car-pool drivers were pulled over and ticketed for no real reason. People waiting for rides were arrested and fined for vagrancy. MIA paid all fines and tickets from donated money.

On Sundays the churches were filled to capacity. "Nothing's gonna turn us around now," Abernathy preached.

"We must persevere until we are given justice," King preached. "Don't lose faith."

"We will win in the end," preached every black minister in Montgomery.

"Amen," came the overwhelming response.

By the end of the second month, the national news services had picked up the boycott story, and the events in Montgomery were being reported to hundreds of syndicated papers all over the country. Money began coming in from people who supported the boycott. They sent letters giving encouragement. The letters were shared during church services to bolster morale and keep the boycotters' spirits high. The MIA used the money to buy station wagons to be used in the car pools.

Everyone was tense. Tempers were flaring, and angry words were spoken. Somewhere, someone hatched the idea that if Martin Luther King were killed, the problem would be solved. *After all, he was the outsider who had come to Montgomery causing trouble.*

On January 30, 1956, Martin Luther King's house was bombed. His wife and baby barely escaped. When Dr. King arrived at his home, a crowd of blacks had gathered outside. It was an angry crowd, armed and ready to fight at his command. But King didn't give the word for violence. He quoted Scripture and called for peace. "Remember," he said, "if I'm stopped, this movement will not stop, because God is with *this* movement." When King had finished talking, the mood of the crowd had changed. They left feeling uplifted. Montgomery officials, who had expected violence, went away amazed. Those who saw him control the crowd with words of compassion and love knew then that M.L. King was not just an ordinary leader.

"Black Moses" was the name people began calling Martin Luther King. In Atlanta, Daddy King was proud of his son; yet he felt uneasy and wanted him to leave Montgomery. But deep down, Mike King knew his son wouldn't leave until his work was done. He knew, because his son was like him. . . and he wouldn't leave.

Dr. King may have been able to stay calm in public, but when he saw the gaping hole in his living room wall, he panicked. The possibility of his own death was not frightening, but he didn't want his family hurt. He went to the police department and applied for a gun permit. His reasons were legitimate, but of course his application was denied.

The next day local newspapers blasted him for "talking

out of both sides of his mouth." He was supposed to be "the leader of nonviolence, yet he had asked to carry a gun." King realized immediately that he had made a mistake. It was very tempting to respond to violence with violence. How could he arm himself and ask others not to do the same thing? He truly believed that a gun carried long enough would eventually be used. He didn't want to harm anybody. He didn't want anybody to harm him either. How could he protect his family? He installed spotlights around his house and hired a bodyguard to protect his wife and baby.

Martin Luther King never again applied for a gun permit, nor did he carry a weapon of any kind, no matter how many threats were made on his life.

The Montgomery struggle was a long and bitter one. Three months passed... six months... eight months.... City officials had used every trick in the bag, including getting blacks to sign a phony agreement. It didn't work. The people knew that unless Dr. King signed the agreement, it wasn't valid. When that didn't work, Montgomery city officials pressed charges against King, Abernathy, and the other MIA leaders for interfering with normal city operations. They also filed an injunction to stop the operation of the car pool, which was said to be operating as "a transit system without a license and therefore illegal." Both cases were pending in the Montgomery courts.

Eleven months had passed. By November 1956, the boycotters were tired of being harrassed by the police, fined, and jailed. The leaders were exhausted too. Dr. King was frustrated. There had been no new breakthroughs in negotiations, and now the car-pool case was ready to be heard. If the judge ruled against MIA and they lost the right to operate the car pool, King was sure the boycott would end. The people had endured enough.

King was feeling particularly low the morning the car-pool case was to be heard in an Alabama circuit court. The judge was deliberating the legality of it when Dr. King was given a message by a reporter. He unfolded the note, which read:

The United States Supreme Court today affirmed a decision of the special three-judge U.S. District Court in declaring Alabama's state and local laws requiring segregation on buses unconstitutional.

The Supreme Court had acted without listening to any argument; it simply said, "the motion to affirm is granted and the judgment is affirmed." The Alabama judge passed sentence that the car pools were illegal, but it didn't matter. The Supreme Court had held that segregation on buses was illegal. MIA had won.

It was over. They had won! King sat speechless. Suddenly he felt very, very tired. He found Coretta, who was seated in the back of the courtroom. They hugged each other and then went home. The long battle in Montgomery was over. . . but for Martin Luther King, Jr. and his family, it was just the beginning of many such battles.

Chapter 5

PRACTICING WHAT IS PREACHED

We are not come to wage a strife
with swords upon this hill:
it is not wise to waste the life
against a stubborn will.

"The Day-Breakers" by Arna Bontemps

King had anticipated a violent reaction to the court order. One week after Montgomery buses were desegregated, violence erupted. Abernathy's home and church were bombed; King's front door was shotgun blasted; buses were attacked and overturned by angry mobs who refused to accept the Supreme Court ruling. But there was no counterviolence. With the help of MIA ministers, black bus riders had been trained in nonviolent responses.

The weeks before the buses were integrated, Dr. King and his people worked diligently to complete the training. The guidelines were based on the "Love Power" philosophy:

If cursed, don't curse back.
If stricken, don't strike back.
Show love and goodwill at all times.
If another person is being
bothered, don't help them.
Instead, pray for the person doing the bothering.

The nonviolent reaction to violence was effective. In time Montgomery settled down; the buses were integrated. The Montgomery success encouraged ministers in other southern states to try similar boycotts to bring about needed changes.

In January 1957, Reverend C.K. Steele of Tallahassee, Florida, called for a meeting of southern black ministers to keep the momentum of the Montgomery success going.

King and Abernathy attended the meeting in Atlanta, and out of that meeting came the Southern Christian Leadership Conference (SCLC), with Martin Luther King elected president and Ralph Abernathy elected treasurer.

The first action King took as president of the SCLC was to write to President Dwight D. Eisenhower asking for a White House Conference on Equal Rights. The idea was rejected by the president.

After a visit to Africa in the spring of 1957, Dr. King returned to New York where, as the president of the newly formed SCLC, he met with A. Philip Randolph, president of the Brotherhood of Sleeping Car Porters, and Roy Wilkins, national president of the NAACP. They discussed the possibility of a mass march to the nation's capital to emphasize the need for more civil rights legislation.

On May 17, 1957, between fifteen and twenty-five thousand people gathered at the Lincoln Memorial in one of the nation's largest civil rights rallies. The crowd was addressed by speakers from every segment of the population: sports figures, actors, singers, politicians, workers, civic and religious leaders. But, when Dr. Martin Luther King, Jr. spoke he became the undisputed leader of the civil rights movement. From then on the SCLC president was a sought-after speaker. His time was no longer his own.

He had to hurry home from one of his trips to be with Coretta when their son, Martin Luther King III, was born.

When King heard his son cry, he smiled and said, "Now that's the voice of a future preacher." After only a few days of privacy with his family, King was back to his busy schedule. Coretta never complained.

One of his scheduled activities was to promote a book he had written: *Stride Toward Freedom: The Montgomery Story*. The book was released in September 1958, and his publisher brought him to New York for an autographing session at Blumstein's Department Store in Harlem. While he was signing books, a well-dressed black lady came up to him and asked, "Are you Martin Luther King?"

"Yes," he answered and looked up just in time to see the woman strike him in the chest with a letter opener. He remembered thinking, "I'm dying". . . he remembered there was no pain. . . and he was strangely calm. Then he drifted off into a peaceful state of unconsciousness.

Dr. King was rushed to Harlem Hospital where a team of physicians operated for several hours to save his life. A rib and part of his breastbone were removed to free the blade, which was a micrometer from his heart. His doctor told the press, "If he had sneezed, he would have drowned in his own blood."

As soon as King regained consciousness, his first concern was for his attacker. People were amazed. He asked that she not be charged. It was obvious that she was insane.

Mrs. Izola Curry, his assailant, claimed that King was a

Communist who was trying to convert her from Catholicism. She was sent to Bellevue Hospital for examination and was later committed to a state hospital for the criminally insane.

Millions of people prayed for King's recovery. During his ten-day stay in the hospital, a crowd stood outside his room praying and singing. Letters poured in from every corner of the globe, including correspondence from President Eisenhower and Vice-president Richard Nixon.

A letter from a high school student touched him deeply.

Dear Dr. King:
I am a ninth grade student at the White Plains High School. While it shouldn't matter, I would like to mention that I am a white girl. I read in the paper of your misfortune and of your suffering. And I read that if you had sneezed you would have died. I'm simply writing to say that I'm so happy that you didn't sneeze.

Dr. King cried when he read this letter. He hugged his wife, and they both agreed they too were happy that he hadn't sneezed.

After his recovery, King interpreted his close brush with death as God's way of preparing him for a future struggle. He felt inadequate. He wondered whether he was ready for the work ahead. Suddenly, he felt a need to know more about Gandhi, the man who had helped to shape many of his own nonviolent attitudes. It was time for King to go to India.

King eats with his family; a portrait of Gandhi hangs over the doorway.

Two years earlier, during the Montgomery bus boycott, Ragnath Diwaker, a Hindu disciple of Gandhi, had flown to Montgomery to speak to America's nonviolent leader. Diwaker seriously questioned King's commitment to true Gandhian philosophy, pointing out that King had not willingly suffered. King had not fasted; he had not gone to jail. Diwaker pointed out that King wore expensive clothing and owned a car. This Western materialism was inconsistent with Gandhian philosophy that called for sacrifice. Diwaker had invited King to India, but time had not allowed the American to accept.

In February 1959 King visited India. He saw the similarities between the problems Gandhi faced and the problems he faced in Alabama. India's caste system was much like southern segregation. The lower-class Indians, the Untouchables, were not allowed certain social privileges. King nodded his head in understanding.

Gandhi had come from an upper-class family; yet he had adopted an Untouchable child, a daughter whom he loved. To demonstrate the injustice of the caste system Gandhi had taken his "Untouchable" daughter into the temple, where she had been denied. King smiled. "To equal that," he said, "our President Eisenhower would have to take a Negro by the hand and lead her into Central High School in Little Rock."

In India, King confirmed his belief that nonviolence was the *only way* American blacks could conquer what violence could not.

King also understood what Ragnath Diwaker had been trying to tell him. In order to lead a movement of this kind, he had to practice what he preached. He had to be willing to suffer with his followers. King could not strip off his clothing and wear a loincloth as Gandhi had; but he had to be willing to make personal sacrifices.

On his way home King went to the Holy Land, where he visited the places sacred to Christianity. When he returned to Montgomery, he felt fortified. But he had a difficult decision to make.

Chapter 6

NONVIOLENCE ON THE MOVE

I know why the caged bird sings, oh me,
When his wing is bruised and his bosom sore,
When he beats his bars and would be free;
It is not a carol of joy or glee,
But a prayer that he sends from his heart's deep core,
But a plea, that upward to Heaven he flings—
I know why the caged bird sings!

"Sympathy," from *The Complete Poems of Paul Laurence Dunbar*, by Paul Lawrence Dunbar.
Published by Dodd, Mead & Company, Inc., New York, New York, 1980.
Reprinted with permission.

Rev. Martin Luther King made his decision. On November 29, 1959 he offered his resignation to the members of Dexter Avenue Baptist Church. He wanted to return to Atlanta, where he could begin building the SCLC into a strong base of civil rights activities. Speaking to his congregation for the last time, he said, "I have come to the conclusion that I can't stop now...I have no choice but to free you." In January 1960 King left Montgomery.

Daddy King was delighted. Both Martin and A.D. were at home serving as assistant pastors of Ebenezer. But Martin had no intention of settling down into a comfortable position and becoming satisfied. There was too much work that needed to be done.

In Greensboro, North Carolina, February 2, 1960—black college students wanted to end segregation right away.

Four students from North Carolina A & T University walked into a downtown store and sat at the lunch counter. They refused to leave until they were served. When news spread to the students of neighboring North Carolina Central College and Duke University in Durham, other students joined them in what became known as the "sit-ins." Soon, all over North Carolina, black and white students were sitting side by side at lunch counters. They were cursed, kicked, hit, and spat upon; but, no matter what happened to them, they responded nonviolently.

The concept of sit-ins was not new in 1960. Blacks had

conducted sit-ins in 1945 and in 1958. But in 1960, television made people more aware of them. Another difference was that black and white students worked together. King was delighted.

In Nashville, James Lawson, a Ph.D. candidate at Vanderbilt, started giving workshops in protest strategy to Fisk and Tennessee State University students. With the help of C.T. Vivian and John Lewis, Lawson instructed the sitters in using the following nonviolent guidelines:

1. Don't strike back if cursed or abused.
2. Don't laugh out loud.
3. Don't hold conversations with your fellow workers.
4. Don't leave your seats until your leader has given you instructions to do so.
5. Don't block entrances to the stores and the aisles.
6. Show yourself courteous and friendly at all times.
7. Sit straight and always face the counter.
8. Report all serious incidents to your leader.
9. Refer all information to your leader in a polite manner.
10. Remember love and nonviolence.

After being told to "remember Jesus, remember Gandhi, and remember Martin Luther King," the students were sent out to do their work.

Although President Eisenhower signed into law the second civil rights bill since 1875, civil rights activists saw it as

King was arrested for the first time in Montgomery. Coretta stands at right.

Martin Luther King delivers his "I Have a Dream" speech in
Washington, D.C., in 1963.

Leaders of the 1963 March on Washington lock arms as they move along Constitution Avenue. The Rev. Martin Luther King is seventh from right.

Dr. Martin Luther King leads the long delayed Selma-to-Montgomery march. At his right side is his chief aide the Reverend Ralph Abernathy.

Civil rights leaders: From left to right, James Farmer, director of the Congress of Racial Equality (CORE); Rev. Fred Shuttlesworth; Dr. Martin Luther King; and Rev. Ralph Abernathy.

Martin Luther King spoke at the funeral of Jimmie Lee Jackson, who was killed during a civil rights demonstration in 1965.

Young and old, black and white, joined in the Selma-to-Montgomery march.

King walks with James Meredith during a freedom march in 1966.

weak and meaningless. The young blacks called for stronger legislation; and they made it clear they weren't willing to wait another eighty years to get it.

Lawson's group led five hundred students—the largest sit-in ever—into Nashville's downtown area, where they demonstrated for integrated lunch counters, movies, and public facilities. They sang an old labor union song, which became the theme song of the civil rights movement during the 1960s:

We shall overcome,
We shall overcome,
We shall overcome someday.
Deep in my heart, I do believe,
We shall overcome someday.

In Atlanta, King watched the student activities with excitement. He wanted to talk to the leaders, but he had more pressing business.

The state of Alabama had accused King of cheating on his state income taxes. It hurt King deeply. "I'm not perfect," he said. "If I have any virtues, the one which I am most proud of is my honesty where money is concerned." He worried that he would be found guilty. "Even if I am found not guilty," he said sadly, "there will still be those who will doubt my innocence."

Then to add to the distress of the trial, King was accused

of being a Communist. He replied, "I don't need a [Russian] to come over here and tell me somebody is standing on my neck." When King was a student, he had studied Karl Marx, the father of modern communism. He had rejected Marxist philosophy because it denied the existence of God. That still didn't stop the rumors from spreading.

The six-day trial drew national attention. The jury found King not guilty, a first in an Alabama court. An all-white jury had found a black man *not guilty*, when the prosecution wanted him found *guilty*. King gave credit to God and the press. The eyes of the world were watching the outcome. During the trial there was not one shred of evidence to prove King had cheated on his taxes. In fact his defense attorney presented evidence showing that the state of Alabama owed King money!

With the trial behind him, King went back to Atlanta and began building SCLC. The student movement still interested him very much. In April 1960 SCLC sent invitations to sit-in leaders in ten states. They met at Shaw University in Raleigh, North Carolina, and formed the Student Nonviolent Coordinating Committee (SNCC—pronounced "snic"). SNCC was not a part of SCLC but Martin Luther King became the guiding force behind both organizations. The actions of these two organizations, combined with the NAACP and CORE, became the unified forces of the civil rights movement in the 1960s.

In October SNCC planned a sit-in at a major department store's lunch counter in downtown Atlanta. King participated and was arrested immediately. His arrest made headlines.

Nineteen sixty was a presidential election year. John F. Kennedy had been nominated as the Democratic candidate for president of the United States. Richard M. Nixon had been nominated as the Republican candidate. King refused to endorse either candidate. But, there were a number of blacks in the South—of those who could vote—who were Republicans because it was Abraham Lincoln's political party. President Franklin Delano Roosevelt had converted many blacks to the Democratic party, but not Daddy King. He was a Republican all the way—until the 1960 election.

King was in jail. Reporters asked candidate Nixon what he thought about King's arrest. Nixon decided to play it safe. He said, "No comment." Later he issued a statement supporting King and the students, but it came too late. John F. Kennedy had decided to *do* something. First Kennedy called Mrs. King and expressed concern for her husband. Then, he used his influence to get King freed.

Once he was out of jail, King gave credit to John F. Kennedy. While it was not an endorsement, it was interpreted as one. Daddy King announced that he was changing his vote to Kennedy—"Never mind that he's Catholic."

Kennedy won the election in November 1960. Black leaders

felt they had a man in the White House who cared about *all* Americans. President Kennedy appointed many blacks to government positions, but it was the appointment of Robert Kennedy as Attorney General of the United States that would make the difference in the civil rights movement. King and Robert Kennedy kept in close touch with each other, and when possible, "Bobby" did what he could to help.

In April 1961 James Farmer, director of CORE, called King to discuss the idea of challenging segregation on interstate bus lines throughout the South. It was agreed that CORE, SCLC, and SNCC would join forces to conduct what became known as the "Freedom Rides." King was named the coordinator of their combined efforts.

On May 4, 1961 two buses left Washington, D.C., filled with both blacks and whites. They planned to travel through Virginia, North and South Carolina, Alabama, and Mississippi. At each stop the riders planned to get off and integrate the lunch counters and rest room facilities. In Virginia and the Carolinas, they were either served or ignored. Nobody was harmed.

When they reached Alabama, the Freedom Rides became a rolling horror. Outside Anniston, Alabama, the first bus was burned and the passengers were beaten with chains, pipes, and boards. The second bus was also stopped and the passengers beaten. The hoodlums got on the bus and forced the driver to take them all to Birmingham. An angry mob met the bus in Birmingham. The riders were forced off the bus and were beaten again.

King wanted to abandon the Freedom Ride campaign. It was too risky. The SNCC students felt differently. SNCC disregarded King's objections and made plans to conduct another ride to Montgomery, Alabama.

At the Montgomery bus station, the riders were again attacked and brutally beaten—including an observer sent by the Kennedy administration. The administration was forced to do something. Federal troops were sent to control the violence and protect the Freedom Riders.

Early in November, through a strong recommendation from Attorney General Robert Kennedy, the Interstate Commerce Commission ruled against segregation on all interstate vehicles and public facilities. The students saw it as a clear victory, but King took no satisfaction in the victory. It had been too painful. "Freedom has a price. . . a very high price," King had said. The Freedom Rides showed just how high that price could be. It was amazing to King that no one was killed.

At home during the Christmas holidays, King tried to forget about his work and just enjoy his growing family. Yolanda, now called Yoki, was six years old, Marty was four, and Dexter was not quite two. Yoki had seen a commercial on television about Funtown, an amusement park just outside Atlanta. She begged her father to take her there. Later King told an audience that "telling my daughter she couldn't go to Funtown was one of the most difficult things I have ever had to do." King said he reached back into his own history and remembered how Mother Dear had comforted him. "You are as good as anybody," he told his daughter. And he made Yoki a promise. "Someday," he told her, "you'll be able to go to Funtown and anyplace else you want to go in this city. . . 'cause Daddy's working on it." He hugged her and wiped away her tears. Then he dried his own eyes.

By the end of 1962, King had staffed SCLC with the most capable people he could find. Reverend Wyatt "Tee" Walker was the "nuts-and-bolts" man. As executive director of SCLC, Walker was responsible for SCLC's day-to-day operations, which ran like a well-oiled machine. Ralph Abernathy had moved to Atlanta and was pastoring a church and working as King's adviser. King called Abernathy "the best friend I have in the world." Along with Abernathy, King hired James Bevel, Bernard Lee, and Andrew Young as advisers.

During a staff meeting, Abernathy commented, "The only thing blacks and whites share in Birmingham is the sewage system."

"We need to do something about that," King said.

After spending time with Coretta and his new daughter, Bernice Albertine, King turned his attention to Birmingham.

Chapter 7

SUFFER THE LITTLE CHILDREN. . .

They tell us to forget
Democracy is spurned
They tell us to forget
The Bill of Rights is burned.
Three-hundred years we slaved,
We slave and suffer yet:
Though flesh and bone rebel,
They tell us to forget.

"Dark Symphony" from *Rendevous with America*
by Melvin B. Tolson.

Published by Dodd, Mead & Company, Inc. New York, New York
Reprinted with permission

In January of 1963, Rev. Martin Luther King announced that he was going to Birmingham. And in that same month, George Wallace was sworn in as governor. King's purpose was to involve the entire black population in an effort to desegregate Birmingham's public facilities. Wallace had run on the platform that there would be segregation in Alabama "now. . . tomorrow. . . forever!" Bull Conners, the police commissioner of Birmingham, echoed Wallace's sentiments wholeheartedly. He promised that "blood would run in the streets" before Birmingham would integrate.

During an SCLC planning meeting, King's aides and A.D., who was by this time pastor of his own church in Montgomery, laid out the Birmingham strategy. SCLC would work with local leaders to organize boycotts and marches. King decided that he would lead one of the marches.

On Wednesday, April 10, 1963, the leaders of SCLC were given a court injunction ordering them not to march. King and Abernathy defied the order and led a march on Good Friday. They were arrested and jailed. But right away something was different. King was isolated from Abernathy and the other protesters.

Outside the jail cell, he couldn't see his brother A.D. leading more than fifteen hundred protesters in one of the largest marches of the campaign. For the first time, King felt alone and afraid. He didn't know what was going on. What

From left to right:
Adlai Stevenson, ambassador to the United Nations; Dr. Martin Luther King, Jr., president of the Southern Christian Leadership Conference (SCLC); Roy Wilkins, executive secretary of the National Association for the Advancement of Colored People (NAACP); John F. Kennedy, president of the United States; Miss Dorothy Height, president of the National Council of Negro Women; and A. Philip Randolph, president of the Brotherhood of Sleeping Car Porters.

had happened to the others? What was going to happen to him? His cell was dark; a single light bulb swung on a cord over his head. He prayed; he tried to sleep, but the floor was cold. He must have finally slept, for voices woke him. To a black man in jail, the sound of men coming in the middle of the night meant one thing—a lynch mob. He stood to face whatever was to come. But instead of the horror he expected, his jailers gave him a mattress and a pillow and told him that he could call his wife. Why all the kind treatment? he wondered.

King called Coretta. That's when he got his answer. Robert and John F. Kennedy had called her. President Kennedy had promised to call Birmingham. Obviously his call had been effective.

The following day, while his lawyer was visiting him, Dr. King saw an article in the newspaper. Eight white clergymen had written a statement urging local blacks to shun the "outsiders" as mere troublemakers. King read the statement and felt obligated to write a response. The document he wrote in a Birmingham jail has become a classic in protest literature:

You express a great deal of anxiety over our willingness to break laws. This is certainly a legitimate concern. Since we so diligently urge people to obey the Supreme Court's decision of 1954 outlawing segregation in the public schools, at first glance it may seem rather paradoxical for us consciously to break laws. One may well ask: "How can you advocate breaking some laws and obeying others?" The answer lies in the fact that there are two types of laws: just and unjust. I would be the first to advocate obeying just laws. One has not only a legal but a moral responsibility to disobey unjust laws. I would agree with St. Augustine that "an unjust law is no law at all."

King continued by identifying the problems caused by all social injustices. He called for white liberals to speak up. He stated that their silence was more harmful than the cruelty of the racists. At the end of his letter, King begged the clergy to forgive him if he seemed impatient, but begged God to forgive him if he settled for anything less than brotherhood. The letter was sneaked out of jail and was published in journals and newspapers all over the country as "A Letter from a Birmingham Jail."

On Saturday, April 20, King and Abernathy were released on bond. On Monday, King and his colleagues climbed the steps to the Montgomery Courthouse. Over the door were the words, "Equal and exact justice to all men of whatever state or persuasion." Inside the courthouse were signs directing blacks to one bathroom and whites to another. King shook his head. One of his friends whispered to him, "Segregationists would have separate air if they knew how." The guards wondered what could be so funny.

The trial lasted a week. King was found guilty but was

released. Meanwhile, the businessmen of Birmingham were feeling the pressure of the boycotts and the bad publicity. They were showing some willingness to negotiate. But City Hall would not hear of it.

Since his release, King had been working with his advisers on another march. On May 2, more than a thousand excited youngsters—some of them as young as six years old—were allowed to join the freedom march. They assembled at the Sixteenth Street Baptist Church to hear Dr. King. He asked if they were willing to go to prison. "Yes!" they shouted. Then two by two, with an adult supervisor, they went out into the streets. They sang and marched peacefully, but Bull Conners, the police commissioner, was waiting for them.

When he saw the marchers, Conners flew into a rage. "Arrest them all!" he shouted. Policemen arrested nine hundred young people, but took no pride in their work. One officer was heard to say, "Ten years from now, we'll look back on all this and say, 'how stupid can you be?'"

The stupidity of Bull Conners could be matched only by his cruelty.

The next day, twenty-five hundred people turned out for the second day of marching. This time the children's parents joined. Conners was ready. As the marchers turned the corner, they wondered why firemen were blocking the street. "Go back!" yelled Bull Conners. The marchers continued walking with signs reading FREEDOM. "We want our freedom now," the marchers cried.

Conners yelled once more for them to turn back. When they refused, he yelled, "Turn the hoses on!"

The firemen turned their hoses into the crowd. The children were defenseless against the raging water. They were hurled against brick walls, flung into the streets, or knocked into parked cars. Many huddled together trying to protect themselves from the stinging water. Others began to run. Conners released the police dogs, who chased down the fleeing marchers.

"Look at those niggers run!" millions of American news watchers heard Conners shout.

Americans were sickened by the horror unfolding before their eyes. Bull Conners documented how hateful a thing racism really is, especially when disguised as "the law." Birmingham was disgraced before the nation. . . the world.

Some people chose to criticize King for allowing children to participate in protest marches. It was the opinion of one child psychologist that what the children had suffered would be damaging to their well being. King was accused of "misusing the children," but he fired back this response. "Where were you when these same children were growing up in a system that we know is psychologically damaging?" King asked. "Where were your voices then?"

After facing his critics, King turned his attention to his

bedraggled followers. He told his people to face the water, face the dogs. "God is on our side. Don't worry," he said with tears filling his eyes. "We shall overcome!"

Just as King asked, the marchers "turned the other cheek" and prepared to march on the third day. Conners was waiting for them. Boldly, the protesters faced the hoses and the dogs. Hundreds were arrested. When a reporter asked Conners how he could do such a thing, the world watched as he answered, "I'm trying not to shoot the. . . ."

King spoke constantly to his followers, reminding them to remain nonviolent. "We will not hate, but we will not obey a hateful law," he said over and over.

Then on May 5, the Reverend Charles Billups and other Birmingham ministers led three thousand young people on a prayer march to the jail, where scores of people were jammed inside. As was expected, Bull Conners was waiting.

"Go back!" Conners shouted.

"Bring on your dogs," responded Billups. "Beat us. Turn your hoses on us. We're not going to retreat."

"Turn on the hoses," Conners ordered. Nothing happened. The marchers pressed forward holding hands and *praying for the people who were abusing them*!

"Turn them hoses on!" Conners yelled. But the firemen refused to obey his order. The policemen refused to budge. The marchers came forward. The policemen and firemen, some of them crying, parted and let the marchers through.

The nation saw for the first time the power of nonviolence. Unwittingly Bull Conners had exposed the true ugliness of segregation and racial hatred. What he had ordinarily done under the cover of night had been seen by millions in the full light of day. Nobody could say the situation had been exaggerated; news reporters from all the major networks had recorded it as it was happening.

The businessmen of Birmingham were in a dilemma. They might have agreed with Bull Conners in theory, but in practice they saw brute force and violence failing against people who didn't fight back. Something had to be done; so, they called for negotiations to begin as soon as possible.

After meeting with Dr. King and local black leaders, the Birmingham businessmen agreed that lunch counters, rest rooms, fitting rooms, and drinking fountains in the downtown stores would be integrated within ninety days. Within sixty days, black clerks and sales persons would be hired and an interracial committee would be formed to continue to work on desegregation in the city.

Of course there were those on both sides who felt too much had been given... or not enough had been won. But, Dr. King was satisfied with the results. Right then, he just wanted to go home. He wanted to see Coretta and spend some time with his fourth child, Bernice Albertine, who had been born just two-and-a-half months before. Sunday was Mother's Day. King would preach at Ebenezer and hug Mother Dear.

Chapter 8

A SEASON OF SUFFERING

"I'm not walking for myself. I'm walking for my children and my grandchildren."

Quote from an unknown elderly woman upon her refusal to accept a ride during the bus boycott in Montgomery.

Only two days after the Birmingham agreement was signed, the city exploded into violence. Ku Klux Klansmen bombed both the Gaston Hotel, where King had been staying, and A.D. King's house.

King returned to Birmingham and encouraged the black population to remain nonviolent. They listened to him. President Kennedy announced to the nation that he was not going to let extremists destroy the good that had finally come out of Birmingham. He ordered three thousand federal troops to Birmingham. The violence ended shortly afterward.

Robert Kennedy was a strong supporter of civil rights legislation. As a cabinet member, he urged President Kennedy to give his support to and push for a federal law that would integrate public facilities throughout the United States. On June 11, 1963, John F. Kennedy called for the country to fulfill its promise of freedom and equality: "I shall ask the Congress to make a commitment it has not fully made in this century to the proposition that race has no place in American life or law."

As the president spoke to the nation about justice, a Mississippi racist shot and killed Medger Evers, the NAACP field secretary, as he stood in front of his house. "We still have a long, long way to go in this nation before we achieve. . . brotherhood," said King. Evers was another victim of blind hatred.

Nineteen sixty-three was the hundredth anniversary of the Emancipation Proclamation. The leaders of the six civil rights organizations met in New York to plan a massive demonstration in Washington, D.C. The purpose of the demonstration was to show support for civil rights legislation and commemorate the freeing of the slaves. Bayard Rustin, a friend and adviser of Martin Luther King, served as the coordinator.

More than 200,000 people gathered at the Washington Monument on August 28, 1963. It was actually the second gathering of its kind, but it was more widely publicized than the first march of 1958. The participants marched hand and hand to the Lincoln Memorial—a sea of people of all races and religions. Many liberal whites had answered Martin Luther King's call for them to stand up, and on August 28, blacks and whites stood together against a system that preached race supremacy.

Speaker after speaker stepped to the podium and addressed the large, happy crowd. They all had one message— equal justice under the law for all Americans. Finally it was time for Martin Luther King to deliver his speech. He had worked on it for a long while. But minutes before he was introduced, he changed his mind. He put the prepared speech in his pocket and spoke what he was feeling.

King walked to the speaker's platform. He began in the slow deliberate manner that was his style. "Five score years ago," he began, "a great American. . . signed the Emancipation Proclamation. . . . But one hundred years later, we must face the tragic fact that the Negro is still not free."

It was a hot and humid day. The people had been listening to speeches for nearly three hours, and they were tired and restless. But after King's first few sentences, every face turned toward the speaker.

King went on to speak from his heart the well-known "I have a dream" speech. He electrified the crowd with words of hope, words of love, and words of peace.

"I say to you today, my friends, that in spite of the difficulties and frustrations of the moment I still have a dream. It is a dream deeply rooted in the American dream. I have a dream that one day this nation will rise up and live out the true meaning of its creed: 'We hold these truths to be self-evident; that *all* men are created equal.' I have a dream!"

The crowd responded to each "I have a dream" with "Amen, Amen." Every "I have a dream" gave the people hope.

"I have a dream," he said "that my four little children will one day live in a nation where they will not be judged by the color of their skin but by the content of their character."

The people were caught up in the spirit of what King was saying. His dream became their dream too. Some of them had joined hands and swayed to the rhythm of his voice.

"I have a dream, today."

A voice called out, "Dream some more, dream some more."

King then turned the focus of his speech to freedom.

". . . Let freedom ring," he said. The mellow tones of his voice resounded through the audience and touched every heart. "Let freedom ring from the mighty mountains of New York. Let freedom ring from the heightening Alleghenies of Pennsylvania. . . but not only that, let freedom ring from Stone Mountain of Georgia. Let freedom ring from Lookout Mountain of Tennessee. Let freedom ring from every hill and molehill of Mississippi. From *every* mountaintop, let freedom ring."

The crowd responded with shouts and cheers. Then came King's climactic ending, which has become the most quoted part of his speech and the flame that has kept his dream aglow!

"When we let freedom ring, when we let it ring from every village and every hamlet, from every state and every city, we will be able to speed up that day when all of God's children, black men and white men, Jews and Gentiles, Protestants and Catholics, will be able to join hands and sing in the words of the old Negro spiritual, 'Free at last! Free at last! Thank God Almighty, we are free at last!'"

For a moment the crowd stood speechless. Men and women wept and hugged one another. Then, as one, the people raised their voices in a roaring ovation.

But the joy of that moment was soon shattered. On September 15, 1963, news came from Birmingham that four girls had been killed at the Sixteenth Street Baptist Church. The girls had come to Sunday school and a bomb had exploded.

King rushed to Birmingham. (Birmingham was becoming known as "Bombingham.") He was walking through the wreckage of the church when his eye fell on a copy of a Sunday-school handout. On it was the prayer for that day: "Dear God, we are sorry for the times we were so unkind." "How much more suffering?" he asked. "Where will the violence end?"

It was a season of suffering, and the cost of freedom was increasing.

Just a few weeks later, Lee Harvey Oswald shot and killed President John F. Kennedy. To some it seemed that the United States was coming apart at the seams. King and the rest of America watched TV and saw Jack Ruby kill Lee Harvey Oswald. Would this nightmare ever end?

King sat glued to the television watching John F. Kennedy's funeral procession. He turned to Coretta and said, "I'll never live to see forty."

There were others who believed, too, that King was a "marked man." In hushed tones, black people began to say to each other, "*They* are going to kill King next. It's just a matter of time."

In a Missouri prison, James Earl Ray believed Oswald had been paid to kill Kennedy. He wondered how much. A million dollars? "Whoever kills King will make a million, too," one of the inmates said. Ray responded, "That's the million I want to make."

Lyndon Baines Johnson became president of the United States hours after Kennedy was shot. Black people weren't so sure about Johnson at first. He was a Texan who spoke with a drawl. He would have to prove himself a friend. And he did. On November 27, in his first presidential address to Congress, Johnson said, ". . . honor President Kennedy's memory by the earliest possible passage of the civil rights bill for which he fought so long."

Johnson then called all the black civil rights leaders to his office and assured each one personally that Kennedy's dream would be his dream too. He promised to help make the dreams a reality.

The year had been a long and hard one for King, but it ended on a high note. A few days before Christmas, King took Yoki to Funtown. It had recently been integrated. Yoki's eyes brightened when she saw the cotton candy and exciting rides. But she felt especially proud when people said to her father, "Dr. King, we are *glad* to have you here."

Chapter 9

A SHADOW DREAM

If we must die—let it not be like hogs
Hunted and penned in an inglorious spot,
While round us bark the mad and hungry dogs,
Making their mock at our accursed lot.
If we must die—oh let us nobly die—

"If We Must Die," by Claude McKay.
From *Selected Poems of Claude McKay*.

The summer of 1964 was called "Freedom Summer." It was the summer in which CORE, SNCC, and SCLC launched a massive voter registration drive in Mississippi. They expected retaliation from the local hoodlums, but nobody could anticipate what actually happened.

In June, two white CORE workers, Andrew Goodman and Michael Schwerner, traveled to Mississippi to look over the area. They were shown around by a local civil rights worker named James Chaney. Just outside Philadelphia, Mississippi, their car was pulled over by local deputies. The three civil rights workers were never seen alive again. In August their bodies were found in a mud dam on the Tallahaga River. Twenty-one men were charged with murder, but the case was dismissed due to lack of evidence.

King grieved over the loss of the young men. He spoke out louder than ever against hate so strong it could lead people to murder. "We cannot stoop to that level. . . . We must never let ourselves become that sick with hate. . . ." preached King.

By mid-October 1964, he had given a total of 350 civil rights speeches and traveled 275,000 miles. His workday was twenty hours long; still, he made time to preach at Ebenezer at least once a month and to roughhouse with his children in the living room.

Near exhaustion, King checked himself into an Atlanta hospital for a long overdue rest. The next morning, after he had slept a full ten hours, Coretta gave her husband the wonderful news. He was the winner of the Nobel Peace Prize! It took a few minutes for the words to register. Then he shouted for joy. It was the first time he had let himself laugh in a long time.

In December, King and his entire family flew to Norway to accept the award. Daddy King was the proudest he had ever been of his son. King's acceptance speech was short but eloquent. He thanked the Norwegian government for honoring him. Then he told the world, "This prize belongs to all men who love peace and brotherhood."

After touring Europe for a few days, the Kings returned home. Hard work lay ahead.

The first thing King did was divide the $54,000 prize money among the various civil rights organizations.

Meanwhile SNCC students had been registering blacks to vote in Alabama and Mississippi. King and Abernathy decided to go to Selma, Alabama. In February 1965 they led a march to the Selma Courthouse. Sheriff Jim Clark, who rivaled Bull Conners in cruelty, met the marchers and drove them out of town, using cattle prods.

In response, hundreds of civil rights workers came to Selma. For seven weeks men, women, and children were arrested after massive protest demonstrations. King and Abernathy were arrested again. They stayed in jail four days, refusing to post bond.

In order to call national attention to the need for voting

legislation, King organized a march from Selma, Alabama to Montgomery, Alabama. George Wallace, the governor, said it could not—would not—take place. King said it would.

On U.S. Highway 80, Al Lingo's Alabama state troopers waited for the marchers. "Go back," the marchers were told. When they kept coming, the troopers began beating them with bullwhips and hurling tear gas. Andrew Young said later that it was very hard to remain nonviolent, especially when people were being trampled with horses.

Again the news media recorded it all. Stunned Americans wanted to show they were against such cruelty. Thousands of Americans resented the treatment of the marchers. They could not leave their families and jobs, but they took a day and marched in their *own* cities, just to show their support of King and his people.

It was fifty-four miles from Selma to Montgomery. King had been turned around once, but he was determined to complete the march. On March 9, dressed in work clothes and hiking boots, King and Abernathy led fifteen hundred blacks and whites along Highway 80.

After George Wallace had sent delays and court injunctions to stop the march, President Johnson sent the National Guard to protect the marchers. On March 25, thirty thousand people gathered in Montgomery to greet the last of the marchers.

The Selma March, often called the most violent nonviolent

protest in history, had come to a bitter end. Three people had died. Rev. Jimmie Lee Jackson, a young black minister, and Rev. James Reeb, a young white minister, had both been brutally beaten to death by racists. Mrs. Viola Luizzo, a white Detroit housewife, had been shot after returning from the march. King mourned all three deaths but still asked his followers to remain faithful to the nonviolent philosophy.

After Selma, President Lyndon Johnson ordered the Justice Department to prepare a strong Voting Rights Act. Johnson presented it to Congress in person. His speech was televised, and millions of Americans, many of them crying, listened to the President. "It is wrong. . . to deny any of your fellow Americans the right to vote. . . . All of us must overcome the crippling legacy of bigotry and injustice. And we shall overcome!"

On August 6, 1965, Martin Luther King was in the White House when President Johnson signed the bill. There would be no more literacy tests. Blacks were guaranteed the right to vote!

Five days later, on August 11, the Watts Riot began in Los Angeles, California. No one is sure how it started. A minor traffic violation turned into a police-citizen confrontation that exploded. Pent-up frustration, anger, and hostility resulted in days of looting and rioting.

It shocked all America, but it was devastating to King. To hear young black rioters yelling, "Burn, baby, burn!" greatly distressed King. In the northern ghettos, black unemployment was high; youngsters dropped out of school as soon as they could, and those who stayed received only a second-rate education. Families lived crammed in one- and two-room apartments, where roaches and rats slept with the children. It was a place that bred violence.

Northern blacks had a different set of racial problems. In the South, segregation denied black people their basic legal rights; in the North, isolation and neglect denied ghetto dwellers basic human rights. A young rioter told King, "We got the right to eat in every hamburger joint in town, but we ain't got no job!"

"Can't you see violence doesn't work?" said King.

"Yes it does," argued the young rioter. "We got noticed!"

NOTICED!

King realized that as a civil rights leader he had forgotten the northern cities. He vowed to do something to help.

The summer of 1966 was called "the long hot summer." Northern cities burst into flames as angry ghetto dwellers rioted. When asked why they burned their own houses, one rioter answered, "These rat holes need to be burned." There were many people who agreed. Martin Luther King did not. He went to Chicago and tried to bring about better housing, more jobs. But he could not sell his nonviolent ideas to the new militant blacks.

Meanwhile, James Meredith, the first black student to

enroll at the University of Mississippi, decided to walk the 210 miles from the Tennessee border to Jackson, Mississippi as a form of protest. On the first day of his walk, Meredith was shot and taken to a hospital in Memphis.

Civil rights leaders Stokley Carmichael, the new president of SNCC; Floyd McKissick, the director of CORE; and Martin Luther King of SCLC met in Memphis. The plan was to finish Meredith's march.

Carmichael came to King. He didn't feel whites were needed in the march. McKissick agreed. King disagreed and insisted that the civil rights struggle was not exclusively a black problem, but an American problem. All Americans had to be a part of the solution.

The march took place in spite of threats on King's life, but the real threat was the split that was beginning to take place between the three civil rights leaders.

The group marched into Greenwood, Mississippi, and gathered at a local park. Carmichael mounted the platform and made his "Black Power" speech. "I've been arrested twenty-seven times," said Carmichael, "and I ain't going to jail no more!"

That night King spoke to McKissick and Carmichael. "Power is what counts," argued Carmichael.

"Yes, power earned by determination and creative endeavor, not negative power," said King.

They did not agree; in fact, that night the long relation-

King talks to supporters during a rest on the Mississippi march.

ship between SNCC and SCLC ended. It just wasn't official yet.

The march continued, but the marchers didn't know that trouble was brewing. In Philadelphia, Mississippi, King conducted a memorial service for Chaney, Schwerner, and Goodman, the civil rights workers who had been killed there in 1964. A crowd of whites encircled the marchers and beat them with hoses and axe handles.

In the end, after being teargassed and beaten, Floyd McKissick of CORE shouted, "Never again!" He promised he would never tell his people not to defend themselves.

"We got guns, too!" shouted Carmichael.

Dr. King warned, "You'll never win with violence."

Carmichael called out, "Black power!"

Following Selma, Dr. King went back to Chicago to continue his work there. He took his family with him this time. After two months, the personalities of his children changed drastically. They became fussy, angry, hostile, and disobedient. They had no place to play; the apartment was hot.

King decided to send them back to Atlanta. The Kings had the money to free their children from ghetto living. What about those who didn't?

King saw the problem as economic. Black people were poor, but there were a lot of poor people in America. King decided he would lead a poor people's march on Washington, much like the march of 1963.

He also believed that as a Nobel Prize winner he should speak out against the war in Vietnam.

These two positions made him a very unpopular man with President Lyndon Johnson. Johnson felt King had betrayed him. The president felt that because he had pushed for civil rights legislation, King owed him his loyalty on the war issue. King answered that he was not against Johnson, but against the war. Unfortunately Johnson didn't accept that explanation. King and Johnson became political enemies.

There were others who didn't agree with King's position. Many blacks and whites felt he had overstepped his "place." Still he clung to his ideas. Some of his *friends* began to criticize him. "The war is not a black problem."

King returned to Atlanta after working long hard hours to bring about only a few housing code changes in Chicago. He was feeling tired and rejected. On a February Sunday, the topic of Dr. King's sermon was his own death. "I'd like on that day for somebody to say that Martin Luther King, Jr. tried to love somebody. . . ."

Chapter 10

GO DOWN, DEATH

"Like anybody, I'd like to live a long life.
Longevity has its place. But I'm not concerned
about that now. I just want to do God's will.
And He's allowed me to go to the mountain.
And I've looked over. And I've seen the
Promised Land. I may not get there with you.
But I want you to know that we as a people
will get to the Promised Land. . ."

Excerpt from Martin Luther King's last public speech

At the beginning of 1968, Martin Luther King was a very tired man. For nearly thirteen years, he had lived on airplanes and slept in unfamiliar hotel rooms. He was tired of never having enough time with his family. He was tired of always having his words analyzed, criticized, and very often misunderstood. He was tired of never having any privacy. He was tired of always having his every footstep monitored by the FBI.

At the beginning of 1968, Martin Luther King was a very depressed man. Was his work making a difference? Those who were closest to him assured him that it was. Still his spirits could not be lifted. There were so many doubts.

"Have all my efforts been in vain?" he asked.

At the beginning of 1968 Martin Luther King was a very tired and depressed man. Yet he continued because, through it all, he was convinced that no cause is ever won without great sacrifice. His reward could not come from mankind.

Ralph Abernathy convinced his friend to take a vacation. The Kings went away for a few weeks. But 1968 was an election year, and King was very interested in the outcome.

Robert Kennedy was challenging Lyndon Johnson for the Democratic nomination for president. King saw Kennedy as a potential ally. It was not only their shared dislike of Johnson that made them friends, but their common interest in poor and powerless people all over the world.

Both King and Kennedy opposed the Vietnam War. Also

King was very happy to see Kennedy taking his campaign to the migrant workers in California, to the Indian reservations in the Southwest, to the Mississippi Delta, and to the northern ghettos where poverty was staggering.

Wherever Kennedy went people responded to him positively. One observer noted, "Kennedy had this fantastic ability to communicate hope to some pretty dejected people."

Whether or not Robert (Bobby) Kennedy would have won the presidential election of 1968 is a matter of speculation. At the time Martin Luther King was optimistic about his chances. If Kennedy won the election, King felt, he would have a friend in the White House who shared his concerns.

But, interested though he was in Kennedy's campaign, King had an appointment to keep in Memphis, Tennessee. The call was from an old friend, Rev. James Lawson, one of the leaders of the Nashville sit-ins back in 1960. Rev. Lawson was pastor of the Centenary Methodist Church in Memphis and was still very much involved in the civil rights movement. King listened as Lawson explained the situation. Thirteen hundred black sanitation employees had gone on strike because they wanted to be represented by a union. They also asked for better working conditions, along with better and equal wages.

Although King was deeply involved in planning the Poor People's March on Washington, he said to his staff, "These are poor people. If we don't stop for them, then we don't need to go to Washington. These are the people we are going there for."

Two days later King spoke before seventeen thousand people at Mason Temple in Memphis. He told them that on Friday, March 22, 1968, they were going to march downtown in support of the sanitation workers. He urged blacks to boycott their jobs and all students to stay away from school on that day. "They will hear you if you walk together hand in hand."

King decided to lead the march himself. He was unaware that a group of Black Power Youth were determined to challenge the elder black leadership in Memphis. They were passing out instructions about how to make firebombs. "You gonna need them before it's over," they shouted.

King knew nothing about this movement, and neither did his advisers. But he was even more unprepared for what he found in Marx, Mississippi.

King had gone on to Marx, with the intent of returning on the twenty-second for the march. There he saw hungry black children with their bellies protruding. "How do you live?" he asked. "Oh, we pick and eat berries during the season, then we hunt rabbits. Most of the time we just don't eat."

King saw illiteracy and poverty as he had never seen it before. He wept. Then he promised to take those people to Washington to show Congress and the president that there

Thousands gathered before the Clayborn Temple A.M.E. Church in Memphis before the mass march led by Dr. Martin Luther King, Jr. Later this march turned into a riot.

was hunger and starvation in America. "Bread, not bombs!" he shouted.

Memphis was struck by a snowstorm, and the march had to be rescheduled for the following Thursday.

Meanwhile, King went to New York to talk with his planning committee. There he met with his old friend, Bayard Rustin. Bayard later said how concerned he was about his friend; something was wrong. In fact, all of King's friends saw a change in his attitude. They couldn't figure it out. He seemed tired, but much more than that—he was preoccupied with death.

On March 25, King was back in Atlanta. His advisers warned him not to go to Memphis and to give up the Washington march. They were sure that violence would result.

On March 28, King was back in Memphis to lead the Sanitation Workers March. He and Abernathy walked at the head of the line. Then they heard the shattering of glass. Black teenagers had begun breaking windows, throwing stones, and looting. King said, "I will never be in front of a violent march." He and Abernathy climbed into a car, and a motorcade tried to lead them back to the Lorraine Motel, where they were staying. The streets were blocked, so they were taken to the Holiday Inn Rivermont Hotel in downtown Memphis. King went to his room and switched on the television set.

Everything was wild. When the violence ended, a teen-ager had been killed by the police, sixty people had been injured, and more than a hundred stores had been damaged. National Guardsmen were called in to patrol the city. King told Abernathy that maybe he should step aside and let the people be violent. But he countered his own argument. "Violence is not the way," he insisted. "It has never worked. It never will!"

King was deeply depressed by what he saw from his hotel suite, but he was even more upset when he saw the newspapers the next day. The press suggested that King "had run out" on his people by leaving the site of the march "hastily." King spoke to the press and told them that he hadn't run, but that he wasn't going to be a part of any violent action. Afterward King told his friend, "Get me out of here, Ralph." Abernathy said later he had never seen Martin so upset.

King had been associated with violence, even though he had had no part in it. He decided to go back to Atlanta to talk it over with his advisers.

Two of King's advisers, James Bevel and Jesse Jackson, began talking against the poor people's Washington march, but King didn't want to discuss Washington. His mind was made up on that issue. Memphis was the question. But Bevel and Jackson continued to discuss the march. King spoke harshly to young Jesse Jackson. It was totally out of character for Dr. King to embarrass his advisers. Everyone knew that King was very tense.

His spirits lifted somewhat when, later that evening, he listened to President Johnson tell America that he was not going to run. "I shall not seek and I will not accept the nomination of my party for another term as your president," said Johnson.

King was astonished. Could he believe that? Or was it a Johnson political trick? King returned to Memphis feeling hopeful.

At the Lorraine Motel, King and Abernathy checked into Room 306, which overlooked a parking lot and a covered swimming pool. There were the usual police cars, news reporters, and, of course, the ever present FBI observers.

The march was to be on Friday.

By late afternoon, King's mood had changed to match the weather. Tornado warnings were posted, and by nightfall a heavy rain was pummeling the city. King was to speak at Mason Temple again, but he told Abernathy he didn't want to go. "They're coming to hear you, not me," said his friend. Abernathy persuaded King to go by being a good listener. He listened as Martin told him, "I am here in Memphis for the same reason the Good Samaritan stopped to help the man in need." By that time Martin had begun to dress.

Like his first speech at Holt Street, King hadn't prepared. He just talked from his heart. At the end he said, "Now it doesn't matter. It really doesn't matter what happens now. . . . Because I've been to the mountaintop. Like anybody, I'd like to live a long life. Longevity has its place. But I'm not concerned about that now. I just want to do God's will. And He's allowed me to go to the mountain. And I've looked over. And I've seen the Promised Land. I may not get there with you. But I want you to know that we as a people will get to the Promised Land. . . ."

As his advisers listened, they were shocked. Was he saying good-bye? Eerie. . . morbid. . . inspired. . . fantastic. . . King's last public speech had varying effects on different people, especially in the light of what happened in less than twenty-four hours.

"So I'm happy tonight. . . . With this faith, we will be able to achieve this new day, when all God's children—black men and white men, Jews and Gentiles, Protestants and Catholics—will be able to join hands to sing with the Negroes in the spiritual of old, 'Free at last! Free at last! Thank God Almighty we are free at last!' "

Many who heard this speech believed that King must have known that death was near. He was ready. Death was coming, "coming like a falling star."

That night King stayed up until after 4:00 A.M. talking to A.D., his brother. Abernathy woke him the next day. "Come on," he said, "Wake up. We have things to do!"

King met with various leaders and made plans for the

upcoming march. He talked with the Invaders, the black militant group who had helped get the violence started in the first march. They gave their tentative support for the march, but wouldn't promise anything beyond that march. When King tried to explain to the Invaders the futility of violence, they seemed disinterested.

Back in Room 306, King ate a big lunch. Then he and A.D. called Mother Dear.

Their plans for later that evening were to go to Samuel Kyles's home for dinner. King was always leery about eating out. He liked to enjoy his meals and asked Abernathy to call and ask what was for dinner. "Soul food," answered Mrs. Kyles. King clapped his hands and smiled. "Greens, chitterlings, and corn bread. Pig feet too!" Abernathy called out.

"I can't stand it! I'll be there in a minute," King said laughing. Abernathy thought how good it was to hear him laugh.

Around 5:30 P.M. on April 4, Samuel Kyles arrived at the Lorraine Motel. Kyles teased King about his earlier call, but they laughed. Everybody knew King's appetite and his love of "down home" food. It was time to leave, but Abernathy went back into the room to put on some after-shave.

Dr. King went out on the balcony with Kyles. Kyles started down the steps, but King leaned over the railing to speak with Andrew Young and Solomon Jones, his chauffeur. Then King saw Jesse Jackson.

"Jesse," Dr. King called out. "I want you to go to dinner with us tonight." He spoke affectionately to Jackson, who realized that King was, in his own way, apologizing. "No blue jeans, all right?"

"Right, Doc," Jackson answered.

Then for a moment King stood on the balcony. Abernathy was coming out of the door. A loud crack split the air. Everybody knew it was a gunshot. Abernathy fell to the floor. He thought King had dived to safety too, but when he looked, he knew his friend had been shot. People began screaming.

Immediately, a special news bulletin reported that Martin Luther King had been shot at the Lorraine Motel. The world waited in hopeful prayer. At St. Joseph's Hospital Dr. Martin Luther King was pronounced dead at 7:05 P.M.

He had once told his wife that he would never live to be forty years old. He was thirty-nine at the time of his death.

Coretta King and her four children arrived in Memphis the next day, having been flown to Memphis on a plane provided by Robert Kennedy. King's funeral was planned for April 9, 1968.

But there was some unfinished business. On April 8 Coretta King led the march that became a memorial to her slain husband. Afterward she flew with her husband's body back to Atlanta.

Daddy King was grief stricken. "My son," he cried, "the son who had brought me such joy. . . . I jumped up in the hall

Mule-drawn caisson bearing the body of Martin Luther King moves up Auburn Avenue toward downtown Atlanta.

outside the room where he was born and touched the ceiling—the child, the scholar, the preacher. . . all of it was gone."

Meanwhile the rest of the country went into trauma.

Ironically, the country responded to King's death with the one thing he abhored: violence. City after city exploded with grief. Angry black youth released their fury in violence. They would not be silent. They burned and looted in the name of a man who had asked to be remembered as a man of peace.

On April 9, 1968, in Atlanta, Ralph Abernathy officiated at the funeral of his friend. One hundred thousand people surrounded Ebenezer. But obvious was the absence of President Johnson and Lester Maddox, the governor of Georgia. Maddox had refused to close the schools and argued that the flag should not be lowered to half-staff.

Dr. DeWolf, King's professor at Boston University, and Dr.

Mrs. Coretta Scott King, assisted by her son Martin Luther King III, places a wreath at the grave of her husband on the tenth anniversary of his death. Her daughter Bernice is standing next to her. At right are Mrs. Christine Farris, sister of the slain civil rights leader, and his father Martin Luther King, Sr.

Mays from Morehouse spoke during the ceremony. Mays said, "God called the grandson of a slave on his father's side and said to him: 'Martin, speak to America about war and peace, about social justice and racial discrimination; about its obligation to the poor; and about nonviolence as a way of perfecting social change in a world of brutality and war.' "

Now the voice was silenced, and the world mourned.

James Earl Ray, a hard-core racist and prison escapee, was arrested in London, England, on June 8, 1968. He was charged with the murder of Martin Luther King, Jr. and was brought back to the United States to stand trial.

Adding to the turmoil of the times, Senator Robert Kennedy had been shot on June 5 in California. Just after winning the California Democratic primary, Senator Kennedy was leaving through the kitchen hallway of his Los Angeles hotel when a man, later identified as Sirhan Sirhan, a twenty-four-year-old Jordanian immigrant, raised his gun and shot the senator at close range. Twenty hours later, Robert Kennedy died.

Martin Luther King—now Robert Kennedy! Would the horrors never end? It was almost too much to bear. Americans were shocked and angered by the senseless killings. To black Americans it was a particularly bitter loss. Many took it personally.

"*They* are going to kill anybody who stands up for us," the blacks cried out in despair. The use of "they" suggested a widespread belief that King and Kennedy were not really killed by individuals. Many people believed that behind their deaths were a group of unknown, but very powerful, people—a conspiracy. The "conspiracy theories" were rapidly accepted by a number of people in important positions. They pushed for an investigation.

James Earl Ray was tried and convicted of first degree murder. Ray's testimony added to the conspiracy question. He maintained that he had been framed. A mysterious man by the name of Raoul, a French Canadian sailor, was, according to Ray, the real murderer of Martin Luther King. Raoul, to this day, has never been found.

There was one investigation after King's assassination and another one some years later. Neither investigation turned up evidence to prove the conspiracy theory, leading some people to conclude that Ray acted alone. On the other hand, there was no positive proof that there wasn't a conspiracy. If there was one, as many people (including members of King's family and his close advisers) believed then and still believe, the conspirators covered their tracks very well.

The same questions remain. Did Ray act alone? Or was he part of a larger, more complicated assassination plot? We may never know.

Then, again we might. As Martin Luther King was so fond of quoting from William Cullen Bryant, "Truth crushed to earth will rise again."

Epilog

YOU KNOW A TREE BY THE FRUIT IT BEARS

Tomorrow,
I'll be at the table
When company comes.
Nobody'll dare
Say to me,
"Eat in the kitchen,"
Then,
Besides,
They'll see how beautiful I am
And be ashamed—
I, too, am America.

"I, Too, Sing America" by Langston Hughes.
From *Selected Poems of Lanston Hughes.*

Published by Alfred A. Knopf, Inc. New York, New York, 1959.
Reprinted with permission.

Before his death in 1968, Martin Luther King, Jr. had doubts about whether his work—his life—had been worthwhile. There were reasons for his despair.

First, the nonviolent civil rights movement was being challenged by youth who believed in violence. They also advocated living separately from whites. Secondly, King had been harrassed by the FBI for over six years. He had been accused of being a Communist, a troublemaker, and an "Uncle Tom." Yet King never gave up. He never gave up because of his faith in God. He hoped that one day he would be remembered, not for the speeches or the prizes he had won, but for the good he had done.

"You know a tree by the fruit it bears" is a saying based on a passage from the Bible. King knew its meaning well: a person's deeds tell us what kind of person the individual is.

Martin Luther King, Jr. was born. He died. But, while he lived, he helped make living better for a lot of people. Look around and see the good things that have come from King's life. All over America, from the Mississippi Delta to the Canadian border, from the Atlantic Ocean to the Pacific Ocean, people of all races are enjoying the experience of playing together and working together—of really living together.

You know a tree by the fruit it bears. The fruits of Martin Luther King's tree are bountiful.

Martin Luther King, Jr. 1929-1968

1929 Stock market crashes. Depression begins. Martin Luther King born. In Mexico, the National Revolutionary Party is founded. In Germany, Heinrich Himmler becomes head of the S.S. of the Nazi Party.

1930 Depression worsens. Vannevar Bush pioneers the computer. Nazi Party dominates German politics. Depression is worldwide. Gandhi leads protest against salt tax in British-ruled India.

1931 British Commonwealth of Nations is established. Japanese invade Manchuria.

1932 Franklin Delano Roosevelt becomes president. Hitler increases power in German parliament. Japanese take over Manchuria.

1933 Federal work programs started. Hitler establishes dictatorship. Spanish government puts down rebellion.

1934 Independence granted to the Philippines, to begin in 1946. King joins his father's church. Lazaro Cardenas becomes president of Mexico. Italians and Ethiopians fight in eastern Africa. Chinese Communist leader Mao Tse-tung leads followers on "Long March" across 6,000 miles of China.

1935 Social Security Administration is founded. King enters an all-black grade school. Hitler re-arms Germany. Nuremberg Laws deny German Jews civil rights. Persia's name changed to Iran.

1936 Minimum wage established for companies with government contracts. President Roosevelt is reelected. Hitler and Mussolini (Italy) sign alliance. Spanish Civil War begins. Arab High Commission is formed; it is against Jewish claims in Palestine.

1937 Supreme Court declares Social Security Act and other New Deal programs constitutional. Golden Gate bridge completed. Neville Chamberlain, British prime minister, tries to prevent war with Germany and Italy. Japanese invade China.

1938 House Committee on Un-American Activities investigates subversive groups such as the Communists, Nazis, etc. Germany invades Austria and occupies Sudetenland (part of Czechoslovakia). Chinese set up capital in Chungking, safe from Japanese.

1939 President Roosevelt declares U.S. neutrality. Hattie McDaniel is first black to win an Academy Award, for *Gone with the Wind*. Nazis invade Czechoslovakia and Poland. World War II begins. Russia invades Poland.

1940 U.S. aids British war effort. Selective Service System (draft) established. Richard Wright, black author, publishes *Native Son*. Germany conquers France. Italy declares war on Britain and France. Germans bomb London. Churchill becomes prime minister of England. Japanese take French Indochina.

1941 Japanese attack Pearl Harbor, Hawaii (Dec. 7). U.S. declares war on Japan and Germany. Atomic bomb research begins. Blacks in armed forces in segregated units. TV broadcasting begins. Germans invade Soviet Union (Russia). Germans attack British in North Africa.

1942 General MacArthur and U.S.-Filipino troops retreat from Japanese at Corregidor. King enters Booker T. Washington High School. Leo Szilard and Enrico Fermi split the atom. Nazis begin murdering Jews in gas chambers. British repel Germans in North Africa.

1943 U.S. defeats the Japanese at Guadalcanal. Weapons Laboratory is set-up in Los Alamos, New Mexico (part of Manhattan Project). German army surrenders near Stalingrad. Allied forces invade Italy. Allies capture Japanese strongholds in South Pacific. Chaing Kai-shek becomes president of Chinese Nationalist Republic.

1944 President Roosevelt elected for 4th term. U.S. forces return to Philippines. King enters Morehouse College. U.S. and British forces drive Germans from Rome. Allied invasion of Western Europe. U.S. Marines fight in the Pacific.

1945 General MacArthur liberates Philippines. U.S. invades Okinawa. President Roosevelt dies. Harry Truman becomes president. U.N. is established. Richard Wright publishes *Black Boy*, an autobiography. Germans surrender in Germany. End of war in Europe. U.S. drops atomic bombs on Hiroshima and Nagasaki. Japan surrenders. War ends in Asia.

1946 Philippines gain independence. Admiral Byrd leads expedition to South Pole. Juan Peron becomes president of Argentina. Nuremberg Trials of war criminals begin in Germany.

1947 Marshall Plan aids parts of war-torn Europe. First supersonic flight. Jackie Robinson becomes first Negro to play in major-league baseball. India gains independence and is divided into two countries, India and Pakistan. Dead Sea Scrolls discovered in Palestine.

1948 Organization of American States founded. King graduates from Morehouse College; goes to Crozer Seminary in Pennsylvania. Czechoslovakia and Hungary taken over by Communist Party. Soviets blockade West Berlin. State of Israel is born; Arabs attack it. Gandhi is assassinated.

1949 Breeder reactor developed by Atomic Energy Commission. Soviet Union develops the atomic bomb. NATO (North Atlantic Treaty Organization) is founded. Geroge Orwell publishes *1984*. People's Republic of China is created.

1950 U.S. sends advisers to Vietnam. Senator Joseph McCarthy charges that there are Communists in the State Department. Beginning of Korean War.

1951 King graduates from Crozer; attends Boston University. Twenty-second Amendment limits president to only two terms. Julius and Ethel Rosenberg are found guilty of spying for Russians and are sentenced to electric chair. Churchill becomes prime minister in England again.

1952 Dwight D. Eisenhower becomes president. Korean War ends. King meets Coretta Scott. King George VI dies; Elizabeth becomes queen of England. Mau Mau revolt against British rule in Kenya.

1953 Martin and Coretta marry. U.S. gives financial aid to France to help her repel rebels in Vietnam. James Baldwin publishes *Go Tell It on the Mountain*. Basic structure of DNA is determined by J. Watson and Francis Crick. Death of Stalin; Georgi Malenkov becomes premier of Soviet Union. Tito becomes president of Yugoslavia. The Rosenbergs are executed.

1954 Joseph McCarthy is censured by Senate for his extremist tactics. Martin becomes pastor of Dexter Avenue Baptist Church, Montgomery, Alabama. U.S. Supreme Court rules that segregation in public schools is unconstitutional. Jonas Salk develops injectable vaccine for polio. French defeated in Vietnam; country is divided in two. SEATO (Southeast Asia Treaty Organization) is organized.

1955 U.S. begins to send aid to South Vietnam, Laos, and Cambodia. Rosa Parks arrested. Dr. King leads boycott of segregated buses in Montgomery, Alabama. Albert Sabin develops oral vaccine for polio. Marian Anderson is first black singer to perform at Metropolitan Opera. Dictator Juan Peron of Argentina overthrown. Israel attacked by three neighboring countries.

1956 President Eisenhower is reelected. King's house bombed. Supreme Court rules segregation on buses illegal; bus boycott in Montgomery ends. Anti-Communist rebellion put down in Hungary.

1957 Governor of Arkansas tries to prevent integration at Central High School in Little Rock. Federal troops enforce Supreme Court ruling. King becomes president of Southern Christian Leadership Conference (SCLC); King visits Africa. *Stride Toward Freedom: The Montgomery Story* published. King is stabbed. Civil Rights Act enacted. *Sputnik* I & II, the first artificial satellites, launched by Soviet Union. U.N. forces keep peace on Israel border.

1958 NASA (National Aeronautics and Space Administration) is set up. Explorer I, America's first satellite, is sent into space. Charles DeGaulle becomes French president. Algeria revolts against French rule.

1959 Alaska becomes 49th state. Hawaii becomes 50th state. King visits India. The King family leaves Montgomery and goes back to Atlanta. Fidel Castro comes to power in Cuba.

1960 John F. Kennedy becomes president. Sit-ins begin in South to integrate lunch counters and other public places. Israelis capture key Nazi, Adolph Eichmann, in Argentina and bring him to trial. Sixteen African nations become independent. Cyprus becomes independent.

1961 "Freedom Riders" in the South try to force integration on interstate buses. Black Muslims speak out for black power and separatism. Communists build wall between East and West Berlin. Soviets are first to send man into orbit of the earth. Alan Shepard becomes first American to go into space.

1962 President Kennedy orders blockade of Cuba to force Soviets to remove missiles from Cuban soil. Algeria gains independence from France. Chinese invade India, capture land and call ceasefire.

1963 Rioting occurs after civil rights leader Medger Evers is killed in Jackson, Mississippi. Dr. King gives his "I have a dream . . ." speech in Washington, D.C. Four black girls die in church bombing. President Kennedy is assassinated. The Beatles enjoy worldwide success. Government of Ngo Dinh Diem falls in South Vietnam.

1964 Voter registration drive in Mississippi. Twenty-fourth amendment, making poll taxes illegal in federal elections, is ratified. Tonkin Gulf Resolution gives President Johnson power to escalate America's role in Vietnam War. King wins Nobel Peace Prize. Aleksei Kosygin becomes Soviet premier; Lenoid Brezhnev becomes general secretary of the Communist Part. Jawaharlal Nehru dies in India.

1965 Dr. King leads protest march from Selma to Montgomery, Alabama. He seeks an end to discrimination in voting registration. Black riots in Watts section of Los Angeles. Malcolm X, Black Muslim leader, is killed. Voting Rights Act is passed. Rhodesia declares its independence. Gambia gains independence. India and Pakistan fight over Kashmir.

1966 U.S. involvement in Vietnam increases. Edward Brook of Massachusetts becomes first black senator since Reconstruction. Beginning of Cultural Revolution in China (1966-69). Indira Gandhi becomes prime minister of India.

1967 Peace talks begin in Paris between the U.S. and Hanoi. Antiwar protests begin. Thurgood Marshall becomes first black Supreme Court justice. Nigerian civil war erupts. Nguyen Van Thieu is elected president os South Vietnam. Six-Day War between Israel and several Arab states.

1968 Dr. King is assassinated by James Earl Ray in Memphis; riots break out in protest. Poor Peoples March, originally planned by King, occurs in Washington, D.C. Senator Robert Kennedy of New York is assassinated in Los Angeles. Alexander Dubcek regime in Czechoslovakia is committed to reforms. It is crushed by Soviet invasion. Strikes and student demonstrations threaten DeGaulle government in France. Spanish Guinea gains independence; name changed to Equatorial Guinea.

INDEX- *Page numbers in boldface type indicate illustrations.*

125

ABOUT THE AUTHOR

Patricia C. McKissack and her husband, Fredrick, are free-lance writers, editors, and teachers of writing. They are the owners and operators of All-Writing Services, located in Clayton, Missouri. Ms. McKissack, an award-winning editor, published author, and experienced educator, has taught writing at several St. Louis colleges and universities, including Lindenwood College, the University of Missouri at St. Louis, and Forest Park Community College.

Since 1975, Ms. McKissack has published numerous magazine articles and stories for juvenile and adult readers. She has also conducted educational and editorial workshops throughout the country for a number of organizations, businesses, and universities.

Patricia McKissack is the mother of three teenage sons. They all live in a large remodeled inner-city home in St. Louis. Aside from writing, which she considers a hobby as well as a career, Ms. McKissack likes to take care of her many plants.